Galloway Byways

SECOND EDITION, REVISED AND ENLARGED

BY

JACK HUNTER

with illustrations by Alan Braby

Dumfries and Galloway
Libraries, Information and Archives
2008

First published 2006
Second Edition 2008

Designed by Dumfries and Galloway Libraries, Information and Archives. Set and printed by Solway Offset Services, Catherinefield Industrial Estate, Dumfries for the publisher.

Dumfries and Galloway Libraries, Information and Archives
Central Support Unit, Catherine Street
Dumfries DG1 1JB
Tel: 01387 252070   Fax: 01387 260294
www.dumgal.gov.uk/lia

Libraries, Information and Archives is a section of Cultural Services which is an operational unit within the Community and Customer Services Division of the Department of Community and Support Services.

ISBN 0 946280 80 3

A complete list of our publications is available from the above address or on our website at www.dumgal.gov.uk/lia. Our e-mail address is libs&i@dumgal.gov.uk

INTRODUCTION

The fact that this book's title is a deliberate echo of *Highways and Byways in Galloway and Carrick* does not mean that it aspires to be compared with or seen as a successor to the Rev. Dick's classic, for that work stands alone. The echo should be regarded as an act of homage. However, *Byways* accurately sums up the intention of the present offering. At a time when Galloway titles proliferate, the aim is to offer something different by concentrating on less well known aspects of the province and its inhabitants; in Sir James Barrie's words the book, in terms of its subject-matter, is a "second eleven sort of chap". The material used is either previously unpublished or drawn from works that are unfamiliar or difficult to obtain. Much of it has been provided by acquaintances and by former members of the long-running series of talks *Discovering Galloway from Books*. I have tried as far as possible to acknowledge those oral sources individually but fear I have omitted many names. I hope a collective recognition of indebtedness will go some way to compensate. I also recognise with gratitude the assistance of Stranraer library and cybercentre staff.

Mindful of legitimate local pride, I have endeavoured to give roughly equal coverage to the two former counties that constitute Galloway. Inevitably in the eyes of many readers I shall have failed. I excuse myself in the words of S.R. Crockett in *The Lammas Preaching*: "...he comes frae the Machars, an' kens little aboot the jealous God we hae amang the hills o' Gallowa'".

INTRODUCTION TO THE SECOND EDITION

This edition contains ten completely new articles, enlarging the work's geographical coverage. In addition, responses to the first edition and further research have led to the expansion of eleven of the original articles. Alan Braby has contributed five new illustrations. The result is a book substantially different from the first *Galloway Byways* but still adhering to the philosophy suggested by the title and making use of the same types of source as the original. I am therefore indebted to even more people for sharing their knowledge and memories with me.

For
Sheila, Fraser, and Lindsey

LIST OF CONTENTS

ESSENTIAL GALLOWAY

The Nature of the People 1
The Galloway Macs 3
What's in a Name?.. 5
Our Own National Anthem 7
... and Tartan 8

THE SEA

The Enemy on the Doorstep 9
An Incompetent Louplander 11
Strange Tales from Ardwall Island..12
The Flannnan Isle Mystery: A Portpatrick Connection 14
Port Logan Curiosities..16
The Long Shadow of John Paul Jones 19
Uninvited Guests 20

FARMING MATTERS

Chilcarroch: The Plough and the Poet 23
Sheep with Gold Teeth..25
Mug Sheep and Snap Dykes..26
Remarkable Rhinns Gatepillars 28
A Persecutor of Peat 30
How the Beltie Got Its Belt 31

INDUSTRIES

Tattie Mills...33
Treacle Works 37
The Whithorn Man Who Co-Founded Esso.....................................38
Galloway's South Sea Bubble 40
An Early Wigtownshire Agricultural College 42
The Talented Douglas Family 45
"Gold in Them Thar Hills"...48

TRANSPORT

Lonely Loch Skerrow 51
Bridging the Ken 54
An Inspector Calls..57
The Flying Duchess 58

"KIRK AFFAIRS"

The Bible, Galloway Version 61
The Ken Valley's "Turbulent Priest" (1) 63
The Ken Valley's "Turbulent Priest" (2) 65
Precentors 66
The Queen, the Colonel, and the Kells Minister..68
A Hidden Treasure of the South Rhinns..70
"Bloody Instructions"? 72

FRAE AA THE ARTS

John Nicholson, Literary Entrepreneur..75
Oscar Kokoschka in the South Machars 77
Visitors to Cumstoun (1): The Fugitive...79
Visitors to Cumstoun (2): The Noble Lord 82
Captain Denniston, Raconteur Extraordinary 84
Hugh Foss of Bletchley Park and Dalry 86
Doctor in Wigtown..88
Wandering Willie's Tale: Made in Galloway 91
Musician on the Moors 93

IN THE WARS

Corunna and Corsewall 95
From the Glenkens to Flanders Fields...98
A Family at War 100
Home is the Soldier?...103
The Loch Doon Scandal 104
Bee Pilots 106
When all Roads led to Glenlochar...108

FOLK LORE

Beware the Hare 111

Mottes and Monsters 113

The Witch Woman of Earlstoun 114

The Holm of Dalarran 116

Who Was Aiken Drum? 118

Galloway Galoshans 121

Rowans, Bort Stones, and Adderheads 123

The Real Sir Patrick Spens? 125

MURDER MOST FOUL

Dark Deeds at Glenluce Abbey 127

Foul Play on the Port William Road 129

The Crown Inn Affair 132

NAMES TO RECKON WITH

Galloway's *Titanic* Survivor 135

One of the Few 139

A Stewartry Godmother 141

Kirkcudbright's Forgotten Empire Builder 142

"Postie" Houston, Man of Many Parts 145

Ebenezer Shaw of the House of Shaws 147

Visits from a VIP 148

Galloway's other Linguistic Genius 151

ESSENTIAL GALLOWAY

THE NATURE OF THE PEOPLE

Natives of Galloway like to believe that they have a separate, distinctive identity and this belief was elaborated on by an anonymous local minister at the end of the nineteenth century. He considered that the unique Galloway character is created by the unique Galloway environment : "our terrestrial conditions have the greatest possible effect upon us…my readers will at once admit the profound truth of this in regard to Galloway character and peculiarities" as he put it in the elevated manner of the day. He then went on to define the physical features of the archetypical "Galloway Man" (in those unenlightened, pre-equal opportunities times). This paragon is long, lean, and sturdily built with prominent, weatherbeaten features. His eyes are bright and his lips thin, flexible, and usually firmly closed.

Our author then boldly proceeded to describe the Gallovidian personality. We are, it seems, industrious, independent, and pawkie (from the myriad meanings of that portmanteau word he carefully selected "wily" and "astute"). He suggested this characteristic shows itself in a reluctance to give a direct answer to a question and accounts for the tightly closed lips (to prevent the escape of any unguarded comment). Our conservative nature leads us to cling stubbornly to old convictions; the reverend author commented with evident feeling: "In religious matters the Galloway mind regards change as hardly better than sacrilege." Our hospitable and charitable impulses do us credit. Our former reputation for hard drinking is no longer justified (or, to be precise, was not, at the close of the nineteenth century: a perusal of a local newspaper might question the contemporary validity of the statement.)

Another contribution to Galloway ethnography appears in *Galloway Gossip, The Stewartry*, where we are told that the progenitors of Galloway people pre-date Adam, being mentioned in the first chapter of *Genesis*. Inhabitants of the province are then sub-divided into no less than six ethnic groups with a bewilderment of physical characteristics listed for each. Sidestepping the latter, we find two "breeds" in the hill country, the first the descendants of the Picts and the second, once the tallest people in Europe, of the Caledonians. Moving to the lowlands we encounter a diminishing group, former farmers and Gaelic speakers; then the Fingauls of Norse-Manx descent, found most frequently in the Southerness, Colvend, Borgue, Whithorn, and Kirkmaiden areas; and thirdly the Kreenies or Gossoks, mostly confined to the Rhins of Wigtownshire and, some say, descended from Irish Picts "but A'm no sayin." (wise man!). The final category is "the Farmer breed", possibly descendants of the Angles, certainly not of the Saxons, but in the author's opinion of Dutch origin.

Those finding the above classification lacking in academic rigour may turn with relief to a report submitted to the Ethnographic Committee of the British Association in 1897. Its author, Rev. Dr Walter Gregor, had made an ethnographic study of Galloway covering 116 people in six of the more remote parishes. From it emerged an identikit picture of the typical Gallovidian male and female. The former is 5'8" tall with brown, straight hair, blue eyes, and a straight nose. The female of the species is 5' 3" in height, also with brown hair, with blue or light gray eyes, and again a straight nose.

Seekers after precision will probably stay with Dr Gregor while lovers of the picturesque (and scurrilous) may be drawn to *Galloway Gossip*.

Sources

"Galloway Herd, A"	*About Galloway Folk, 2nd edn* Castle Douglas, 1900
Gregor, Dr W.	*Folklore in Galloway* in *Annual Report of the British Association, 1897* London, 1897 .
Trotter, R. de B.	*Galloway Gossip, The Stewartry* Dumfries, 1901

THE GALLOWAY MACS

"A Galloway Herd" concluded his description of the typical Gallovidian by remarking, "As for his name, it is ten to one that it begins with a Mac" (as we shall see, the odds are in fact considerably shorter). The large number of Galloway natives with names of that type, as well as the names themselves, is a source of astonishment to outsiders. The famous travel writer H.V. Morton was affected in this way, relating how names on shopfronts like McGuffog and the "even less credible" McHarrie made him stare in disbelief. Of course, to locals such names are unremarkable as Morton also noted. However it is unarguable that Gallovidians exhibit an unusually high proportion of "Mac" surnames. A late nineteenth century survey by P. Dudgeon found that in Scotland as a whole 10.5% of surnames began with "Mac" whereas in Galloway that percentage almost doubled to 19.5. Within Galloway itself, surnames of this type were very unevenly distributed with 15% in the Stewartry and a massive 24% in Wigtownshire, the latter evidence perhaps of the very strong Irish influence.

The survey also found that the proportion of "Mac" surnames was at that time decreasing: according to its author 220 surnames found before 1700 were no longer in use after that date. They included examples strange even to Galloway ears: MacBreckic, MacCrochat, MacHeid, MacJedrow, MacOdali, and Macsalnivi. With these in mind it is not difficult to have sympathy for Morton's view that some Galloway "Mac" names sound as if they belong to comic characters in a novel. And it seems as if the decrease may be continuing. Dudgeon's list of "Mac" surnames found from 1700 to 1888 contains many surely no longer in use: MacCaa, MacCrabin, MacElshiner, MacFegan, MacFrizzle. Despite this diminution, however, the Galloway "Macs" phenomenon is still very much with us. A glance at a telephone directory will show an almost complete alphabet within the Mac heading from McAdam to McWilliam.

The author of the 1888 survey makes no attempt to classify the Galloway "Macs", leaving that task to Mrs Maria Trotter, as quoted by her son in *Galloway Gossip, The Stewartry*. We shall follow that example and look instead at Dudgeon's suggestions about the reasons for the phenomenon. He points out that at one time spelling was not fixed but phonetic: a name was written down the way it sounded to the listener. Consequently several seemingly different names may be simply versions of a single one. The example given is the group of surnames McEwen, McGowan, McKean, and McCowan, all seemingly variants of McOwen. It is also claimed that immigrants to Galloway adopted "Mc" in front of their surnames in order to seem local and avoid the dreaded label "Incomers". For the same reason Irish immigrants often changed their "O'" (also meaning "son of") for the more native-sounding "Mc", O'Shane thus becoming McShane. However, it seems that Mr McOlear had not quite got the hang of the process.

Dudgeon suggests that Welsh "ap", equivalent to the Irish "O'" and Scots "Mc", may appear in a few early Galloway surnames like A'Corson and A'Hannay (names of this kind are also noted in *Galloway Gossip*). If correct, this is a valuable reminder that the first form of Gaelic spoken in Galloway was Cymric or Welsh .

The number of Galloway "Macs" may be greater than at first sight appears for Dudgeon claims that when "M'", the equivalent of "Mc", was written carelessly, the ' was omitted so that M'Ilroy was removed from the ranks to become Milroy. On the other hand, local speech habits, still today, decimate the ranks of "Macs" for it is normal in everyday conversation to drop the prefix when referring to one of the clan: "McClune" becomes "Clune".

But what do we make of Mr McNoah?

Sources

Dudgeon, P.	*"Macs" in Galloway* Edinburgh, 1888
"Galloway Herd, A"	*About Galloway Folk, 2nd edn* Castle Douglas, 1900
Morton, H.V.	*In Scotland Again* London, 1933
Trotter, R. de B.	*Galloway Gossip, The Stewartry* Dumfries, 1901

WHAT'S IN A NAME?

Galloway possesses a large number of eye-catching farm names usually of Celtic origin. Most of those are found in Wigtownshire, where the influence of Irish Gaelic was stronger, but the Stewartry is by no means deficient in them. Proof is to be found in the Tarff-Dee valley in the two farms rejoicing in the name of Quintinespie. North Quintinespie stands at the roadside on the A762 just north of Laurieston while South Quintinespie is found immediately south-east of that village, just off the B795 to Greenlaw.

South Quintinespie

According to place-name authority Sir Herbert Maxwell, two possibilities exist for the origin of the name. The first is that it means "The bishop's woods" but the second is more enticing. This suggests "The bishop's dispute" and, if correct, might refer to an incident in 1174 when King William the Lion marched into Galloway with an army to subdue yet another rebellion by his perennially restive, south-western subjects. Tradition says that battle was averted by the mediation of a bishop, who reconciled the would-be combatants although the Gallovidians had to provide a sum of money and hostages to cement the deal.

The name Quintinespie figured in another, more domestic, dispute in 1640 and distracted the attention of The War Committee of the Stewartry of Kirkcudbright, who were already fully occupied trying to provide and maintain the county's contingent of soldiers for the covenanting army in the field against Charles I. They were called upon to deal with George Livingstone of that address and his neighbour, John Gordon of Beoch, two miles to the south, for "committing ane ryot and injuring ane anither". Witnesses claimed that Gordon had struck the first blow but in response to Livingstone's taunts of "Unhonest Beoch and adulterous Beoch". Gordon was fined and briefly imprisoned; the Committee's instruction that he should have no contact "in all time hereafter" with "Margaret Livingstone, spouse to John Merteane," suggests that the "adulterous" epithet   was justified and that George Livingstone had been   defending the family's good name. The latter would be important to the Livingstones for they were well known local figures, owning both Quintinespies for a hundred years.

Sources

Maxwell, Sir H.   *The Place Names of Galloway* Glasgow, 1930
M'Kerlie, P.   *History of the Lands and Their Owners in Galloway Vol. 3*
                         Edinburgh, 1877
Nicholson, J. (ed.)   *Minute Book of the War Committee of the Covenanters in*
                         The Stewartry of Kirkcudbright... Kirkcudbright, 1855

OUR OWN NATIONAL ANTHEM

Residents of Galloway view the long-running debate about a suitable national anthem for Scotland with polite indifference for the principality (to be modest about its former political status) has a "national" anthem of its own in *Bonnie Gallowa'*. This was the creation of farmer's son George G.B. Sproat, a native of Buittle parish, who became the very successful tenant of High Creoch farm on Cally estate just outside Gatehouse. Sproat enjoyed a local reputation as a poet; the collected edition of his work, *The Rose o' Dalma Linn and Other Lays o' Gallowa'* , was published in 1888 with illustrations by his friend the well known Gatehouse artist John Faed.

Nelly Dyson, The Rose o' Dalma Linn (after John Faed)

Bonnie Gallowa' appears in this collection not as a separate poem but in the text of *The Rose*, a long narrative poem: Sproat was taking a leaf out of Sir Walter Scott's book, several of whose best known lyrics are embedded in longer, narrative poems in this way. The plot of *The Rose* is highly convoluted with a surfeit of Victorian sentimentality and melodrama, *Bonnie Gallowa'* playing a vital role in its resolution.. The poem relates the love story of two Fleet valley residents, shepherd's daughter Nelly Dyson, and fisherman Ivan Gray, whose trysting place is Dalma Linn. Their courtship encounters a Himalayan range of obstacles when Ivan incurs the displeasure of The Witch of Girthon. After a long chronological and geographical separation they are improbably reunited on the mean streets of Gloucester, where both are wandering in a destitute state. The means of their reunion is our anthem, sung by Ivan, now a street musician, whereby both song and singer are instantly recognised by Nelly. The couple then return to Anwoth and matrimonial bliss.

A slightly exotic note is added to *The Rose* as, apart from what we now know as *Bonnie Gallowa'*, it is written in the stanza form famously used by the American poet Longfellow in his *Hiawatha*, once staple fare in schools. However the tune is unarguably home bred as it was composed by George F. Hornsby, organist to the Murray family at Cally House, now Cally Palace Hotel.

Sources

Gordon, J.   personal communication
Harper, M.   *The Bards of Galloway* Castle Douglas, 1888

…AND TARTAN

In an era when even football clubs have their own tartans the existence of a Galloway tartan is surely no surprise. Its comparatively modern origin just under sixty years ago in the immediate post-war years is no argument against its authenticity. The weight of evidence shows that tartans indicating membership of a particular, non-military group date from no earlier than the start of the nineteenth century, when they began to be designed for that specific purpose.

The Galloway tartan was devised by John Hannay, a native of Minnigaff, who made his home in the Chelsea district of London, where he had a private chiropody practice. He served as a Chelsea borough councillor from 1945 until his death in 1963 and in 1962 was elected Deputy Mayor. The location of council meetings was perhaps not then as glamorous as it later became: the town hall was situated in King's Road. Hannay was also a leading member of The London Galloway Society and ensured that readers of *The Galloway Gazette* were kept well informed of that body's doings.

His tartan, designed around 1948 and woven at the famous Cree Mills in Newton Stewart, is a district one, intended for people with Galloway connections. It comes in two versions. The hunting or everyday Galloway is predominantly of two subdued hues of green, dark green and moss green, while the dress Galloway is of eye-catching blue and red. The latter has over the years proved the more popular and enduring. Its adoption by Stranraer and District Pipe Band, founded at the time the tartan was created, has ensured for it a high and continuing public profile.

Source

Balfour, L.	personal communication
Hannah, D.	personal communication
Keay, J. and J. (eds)	*Collins Encyclopaedia of Scotland* London, 1994
Macleod, I. (ed.)	*The Illustrated Encyclopedia of Scotland* Edinburgh, 2004

THE SEA

THE ENEMY ON THE DOORSTEP

Surprisingly the international conflict which most directly affected the population of Galloway was not World War Two, in spite of the plethora of military bases here, nor World War One, although a vicious campaign of submarine warfare was fought in the North Channel, and churchyards from the Rhinns to Kirkcudbright record its victims. What brought part of the population of Galloway literally face to face with the enemy was a much earlier event, the series of wars between Britain and France around 1700. During the first instalment, between 1690 and 1697, the French navy established clear maritime supremacy so that French privateers enjoyed a "happy time" round the coasts of Britain with the North Channel one of their main hunting grounds.

A graphic picture of their unchallenged depredations emerges from a claim for compensation lodged with the Lords of the Treasury a year after the war ended. The author was Andrew Agnew, laird of Croach (now Cairnryan) estate on the east side of Loch Ryan, and a professional soldier. He pointed out that during his absence on active service French privateers who "infested the coast of Galloway and particularly Loch Ryan" had ravaged his estate, not only seizing cattle to supplement the shipboard diet but cutting out and carrying away flooring and joists from houses, presumably to effect repairs to their vessels. His terrified tenants had in consequence been unable to cultivate their lands; their fears seem to have been justified for one of them, the tenant of Claddyhouse, had not only had his lands laid waste but he himself had twice been carried off and held to ransom.

Whether or not compensation was paid is not known but the petition had some effect for when war broke out again in 1702 the Scottish parliament requested the Privy Council to establish a garrison armed with cannon on the shores of Loch Ryan to deter the privateers, who were already in the area. The request fell on deaf ears but obviously the situation did not improve for in 1706 Agnew wrote direct to the Privy Council proposing that a fort housing six cannon be built on the Whiteforeland of Loch Ryan (now Lighthouse Point). He also offered to transport the cannon and shot from Dunbarton (sic) Castle and build the fort and associated barracks for the sum of 50 pounds. Lack of a satisfactory reply led to a further request backed up by 31 ships' captains and a reminder that "the Enemy have lately taken ships of great value riding at anchor in the bay of Lochryan".

No evidence exists that the desired fort was ever built; presumably the turning of the tide of war against France eventually removed the threat to the shores of Galloway, which had so unexpectedly thrust its inhabitants into the front line to a degree not experienced since those perilous days.

A possible link with the latter was found in 2007 with the discovery of a low-denomination French coin in a field at Sandmill farm, which lies on the east side of Stranraer on the shores of "the bay of Lochryan". It was identified as dating from the reign of Louis XIV, that is from 1643 to 1715. While professional numismatists are unconvinced, the date of the coin and location of the find make it possible that the coin was dropped by a member of a French raiding party sent ashore for one of the purposes so graphically described by Andrew Agnew of Croach in his unsuccessful compensation claim.

Sources

Pickin, J.   personal communication

Rodger, Edward   *French Privateers on the Wigtownshire Coast* <u>in</u> *Glasgow*
                                  Archaeological Transactions, New Series, Vol. VII, Part II
                                  Glasgow, 19--

AN INCOMPETENT LOUPLANDER

"Louplanders" was the name given in the late eighteenth century to smugglers operating between the Isle of Man and the conveniently adjacent Galloway coast. One notably unsuccessful louplander was Miles Crowe of Kirkcudbright. On one occasion Miles decided to smuggle tea directly into his home town by travelling across from the Isle of Man on a regular passenger ship. He was something of a dandy in his dress and at this time the height of men's fashion was very wide breeches which buckled below the knee. Miles saw an opportunity to be elegantly attired and at the same time dupe the customs authorities. He dressed himself in a pair of the wide breeches and filled them to the waistband with contraband tea. However, as he was disembarking at Kirkcudbright he took too long a stride from the vessel to the quay, the fine cloth of his breeches split, and their whole cargo of tea landed in the water.

The chastened smuggler decided to switch to dealing in spun tobacco. To evade detection while sailing on a regular service he rolled the top half of his body in the sheet of tobacco so that he resembled an Egyptian mummy as he had learned this was the approved smuggling procedure. However he did not know that the proper method was to roll the tobacco on top of the undergarments and instead put it next to his skin with almost fatal consequences. He had not been long on board ship when he contracted a violent fever. The passengers who came to his aid opened his shirt to give him air…and discovered the tobacco. The irate master promptly handed him over to the customs authorities.

Unsurprisingly Miles decided to take early retirement from louplanding and obtained a post on the ferry that plied across the Dee between Kirkcudbright quay and Castle Sod on the west bank. But misfortune followed him into his new job. He died suddenly after a drinking bout and was buried in the town churchyard. Soon, however, rumours spread that Miles's corpse had been removed by the "resurrectionists" for this was the age of the bodysnatchers. No factual basis for this claim was discovered until a criminal called Stewart was hanged in Glasgow in August, 1829. Before his death Stewart confessed that among the numerous people he had killed by poisoning their drinks, afterwards digging up his victims' bodies for sale to university medical schools, was the assistant ferryman at Kirkcudbright, one Miles Crowe. Confirmation came when the grave was opened and found untenanted. It might be argued that as a subject for dissection in the anatomy class the erstwhile, inept smuggler performed a more socially useful role posthumously than he had in life.

Sources

Drylie, J.B.　　　　　*Worthies of Dumfriesshire and Galloway* Dumfries, 1908

STRANGE TALES FROM ARDWALL ISLAND

Of the many smugglers' landing places on the Galloway coast in the eighteenth century heyday of the trade none was more remarkable than that on Ardwall Island, one of the Isles of Fleet in the estuary of that name. The island had the usual amenity of large, stone-lined brandy holes (on its west and southern shores) for storing contraband but unusually entry was by hatch as if into a ship's hold. Even more unusually, in some cases a drystane dyke of large boulders was built over the entrance so that part of the dyke had to be dismantled to give access to the underground chamber. But in the peak years of smuggling the island boasted an even more desirable feature, a tavern. Its patrons must have been almost exclusively smugglers for access to the island from the mainland on foot is only possible for two hours on each side of high tide. Presumably the innkeeper experienced no difficulty in obtaining supplies of alcohol.

The Cuthgar Stone

The tavern occupied a site which had experienced enough changes of use to give a modern planning authority apoplexy. The ground was originally used, from the sixth to the eighth century, to accommodate a small religious settlement centred on a shrine. Excavations in 1964-65 revealed in a tavern wall a stone, dating from the eighth century, inscribed with a cross and inscription. Known as the Cuthgar or Cudgar Stone it is now on display in Dumfries museum. By the thirteenth century the site had been converted to secular use and housed the timber hall of a local nobleman. In its eighteenth century "licensed" premises phase its best known landlord was Irishman Larry Higgins, who lived on the island with his wife for almost fifty years so that it became locally known as Larry's Isle. For most of his residence Higgins eked out a scanty living by farming one of the three or four holdings into which the 40-acre island was divided. Then he suddenly came into money by dubious means connected with a wrecked ship and took over the island tavern. This may have been his undoing for, in spite of his local knowledge, he was drowned one night while crossing between the island and the mainland.

If Higgins's wealth was indeed based on the unholy practice of wrecking, then it is ironical that his tombstone in Kirkandrews churchyard stands beside one to some shipwrecked sailors.

Sources

Thomas, Charles   *Ardwell Isle* <u>in</u> *TDGNHAS, Third Series, Vol. XLIII* Dumfries, 1966

Wood, J. Maxwell   *Smuggling in the Solway* Dumfries, 1908

THE FLANNAN ISLE MYSTERY: A PORTPATRICK CONNECTION

"Though three men dwell on Flannan Isle
To keep the lamp alight,
As we steered under the lee, we caught
No glimmer through the night!"

So begins W. W. Gibson's celebrated poem based on true events on Eilean Mor, one of the largest of the seven, uninhabited Flannan Isles, which lie twenty miles west of Lewis in the Outer Hebrides on Scotland's west coast While the real story is not as sensational as the poem, it nevertheless constitutes an abiding and fascinating mystery, a Scottish, lighthouse-based version of the *Marie Celeste* enigma.

On December 15th, 1900, a passing ship reported that the light on Eilean Mor was unlit. It was Boxing Day before the relief lighthouse tender *Hesperus* was able to land an investigating party on the island. The men found no trace of the three keepers and nothing to explain their disappearance; the kitchen table was set for a meal but the food had not been touched. The only indication of something untoward was an overturned chair beside the table. A minute search of the island yielded no trace of the missing keepers or clue to their fate. So matters remain 100 years later.

But the Flannan Isles and their mystery lie far from Galloway; what is the connection? It is found in the maritime village of Portpatrick and its lighthouse keeper in the mid-nineteenth century, Mr James Beggs, whose son William, born in Portpatrick, followed his father into the service of the Northern Lighthouse Commissioners. By the time of the Flannan Isle incident William Beggs had fifteen years' experience in the lighthouse service, and it was he who was chosen as principal keeper of the team sent to take over at Eilean Mor immediately after the disappearance of their predecessors.

His cheerful disposition and love of nature, particularly ornithology, perhaps made a difficult and unenviable posting tolerable; at any rate Beggs remained at Eilean Mor for five years. And the fact that his son followed him into the same vocation suggests the experience was not a traumatic one. But one wonders what thoughts and apprehensions went through his mind and the minds of his two colleagues during those first days at the end of 1900 when they took possession of the lighthouse so inexplicably and eerily vacated by its previous occupants:

"Three men alive on Flannan Isle
Who thought on three men dead."

However before long the present demanded William Beggs's full attention for in July, 1901, he had to report a mishap to his employers, the Northern Lighthouse Board in Edinburgh. While the keepers were preparing to land stores from the supply vessel at the West Landing by means of the crane half way up the cliff, part of the crane mechanism broke, fortunately without causing any injuries. However the incident must have caused reverberations. In 1898 the collapse of a similar crane at Sule Skerry had killed a seaman on the supply boat and led to a circular emphasizing the need to maintain cranes in good repair and inspect them regularly. In spite of this, at Flannan eight months before the tragedy the crane above the West Landing had suffered an accident while being operated, in consequence of which the operator had been reprimanded for "thoughtlessness at least" and redoubled vigilance in maintenance and operation urged. Now here was more trouble with the same crane and the West Landing was a particularly significant location. It was the only place on the island where any possible clues as to the disappearance of the keepers had been found in the form of broken hand rails on the path down the cliff. Undoubtedly any potential problem with the West Landing crane in December, 1900, would have produced an immediate and urgent response from the keepers.

Surely the chain of events must have raised questions in the minds of William Beggs and his fellow keepers on Eilean Mor as well as at the Northern Lighthouse Board. However the only recorded response of the Principal Lightkeeper was a practical suggestion for adding a piece of equipment to the crane to prevent any further accidents of the same kind. A resolute concentration on practicalities was probably the best way to ensure mental equilibrium on the Flannan Isles in the aftermath of the events of December, 1900.

Sources

National Archives of Scotland	material from Northern Lighthouse Board archive
Rankin, A.	personal communication

PORT LOGAN CURIOSITIES

Port Logan might seem a strange choice for a book titled *Galloway Byways* as its famed botanic garden and fish pond have long made it a tourist attraction, a status enhanced by its recent association with the popular TV programme *Two Thousand Acres of Sky*. However, the village also possesses several little known features well worthy of attention and our concern is with those.

On the beach midway between the community hall and the first houses of the Low Row, between high and low water marks, a shallow arc of stones with a maximum height of about a yard catches the eye. Local tradition says this is a relic of a shipping mishap in the days of sailing vessels. Apparently a vessel called the *Constance* sought shelter in the bay in stormy weather but was driven on to the beach and stranded. After repeated attempts to refloat her had failed, her ballast of stones was unloaded and this succeeded in freeing her. Her crew quickly left the scene of their misfortune without reloading the ballast, which lies on Port Logan beach to this day. Presumably the waves and currents have in time spread out the pile of stones into the shape they now have.

On the north side of the bay, situated on the headland known as the Mull of Logan, stands a conspicuous stone structure. From the village to the south it looks like a slim column but from the east and from out at sea to the west the feature seem to be a small, battlemented tower. Close inspection discloses that the structure is a folly,

Tower on Mull of Logan with hut (reconstruction)

consisting of just the western wall of a tower. It is about 30' wide by 20' high, built of dressed, local stone. On the landward side a shallow, inverted-V groove with its peak about 15' high is probably the slot for a roof, indicating that a hut or shed was built end on to the wall. The lack of foundations suggests that the building was a wooden one, probably for agricultural use.

The "tower" may be the result of Colonel McDouall of Logan, the laird's, desire to see Port Logan rather than rival Portpatrick made the Scottish port for the short sea route with Ireland. In the early nineteenth century McDouall implemented plans drawn up by the celebrated Thomas Telford for a new pier at Port Logan together with lighthouse, sea wall, and access road. It seems possible that the tower was part of this expansion of the port's facilities, its purpose being to identify the position of the harbour to shipping in the North Channel.

The Colonel's plans for Port Logan (or Port Nessock) were not far fetched. The anchorage was for long seen as a serious contender for the role he wished for it. As early as 1715 the Geographer for Scotland, John Adair, stated it was the only place on that coast with the potential for a safe anchorage. And although no regular passenger ferries ever operated out of Port Logan it did enjoy a share in the profitable trade in imported Irish cattle, which peaked in the late eighteenth century with an astonishing 21,500 shipped over in 1796, not for local consumption but for driving to England. While Portpatrick received the bulk of this traffic, a contemporary recalled that for weeks on end the Port Logan road never wanted cattle. And seemingly the Port Logan trade had one special feature. The drovers returning from the south brought with them donkeys, which were shipped over on the cattle boats. The donkey trade was quite a substantial one: it was estimated that in one spell 500 passed through in less than a fortnight. While this may seem a "coals to Newcastle" exercise, donkeys were then the main form of traction in rural Ireland and thus in great demand..

A century after Colonel McDouall had tried to win for his harbour the status of Scottish terminus for the short sea route to Ireland, an even greater prize seemed likely to come Port Logan's way. In 1908 in the halcyon days of the British Empire Sir Andrew Agnew of Lochnaw proudly recorded that the anchorage had been selected as the port of departure for the All Red Route, a proposed land- and sea route to Australia and New Zealand running only to imperial ports and across imperial territory. Sadly for the village the proposal came to nothing and so Port Logan's chance to become internationally known was lost – at least until its recent TV fame.

A more modest claim to media fame may be made on behalf of the former Port Nessock, that of having had one of the oldest public libraries in the area. It was situated halfway along the Low Row, where a house still bears on the fanlight above the front door the legend "Reading Room". This desirable double facility was established in the late nineteenth century by the laird of Logan estate, James McDouall, for the benefit of his tenants. By 1898 the book stock numbered nearly one thousand while a 1908 guide commends it as "a good public library with an ample supply of literature". A contemporary, who holidayed as a boy in the village, testifies to not only the quantity of the stock but also its quality. When the library closed in the 1950's the decision to sell off all the books at a flat rate of two shillings (ten pence) per volume created a miniature gold rush from the ranks of knowledgeable book collectors.

James McDouall's library anticipated the modern emphasis on inclusiveness. At the rear of the building a wooden extension was built to serve as a carpet bowling hall. Bowlers and book lovers unite in remembering the laird's munificence with gratitude.

Sources

Agnew, Sir A.	*Guide to Wigtownshire, 1908 edn* Dumfries, 1908
Cochran, L.E.	*Scottish Trade with Ireland in the Eighteenth Century* Edinburgh, 1985
Corrie, J.M.	*The Droving Days in the South-Western District of Scotland* Dumfries, 1915
Donnachie, I.	*The Industrial Archaeology of Galloway* Newton Abbot, 1971
McColm, S.	personal communication
MacHaffie, F.G.	*The Short Sea Route* Prescot, 1975
MacQueen, J.	personal communication
Scott, W.	personal communication
Torrance, G.	personal communication

THE LONG SHADOW OF JOHN PAUL JONES

Galloway-born John Paul Jones's daring attempt in 1778 during the American War of Independence to kidnap the Earl of Selkirk from his mansion at St Mary's Isle near Kirkcudbright left the authorities in a state of extreme nervousness. This is shown by a document from an archive relating to the Hathorn Stewart family of Physgill estate near Whithorn. Dated September, 1779, the paper is a circular given to John Hathorn of Over Airies and Physgill by the customs and excise officer in Isle of Whithorn. That gentleman had received it from his superior at Wigtown, whither it had been sent by HM Customs in Edinburgh. The document contained disquieting news. An American squadron of four warships under the command of Paul Jones had been sighted off County Mayo in the south-west of Ireland. Its intention, it was claimed, was "to scour the coast and burn particular towns".

In the event Jones did not enter the Irish Sea as he had done the previous year to the disturbance of the Selkirk family breakfast. Instead he sailed round the north of Scotland to harass the east coast of Britain, encounter *HMS Seraphis* off Flamborough Head, and earn immortality. However, the incident raises an interesting question: why did the officer at Isle of Whithorn take the trouble to pass the communication to John Hathorn of Physgill? It may have been because the latter was a commissioner of supply, equivalent to a modern regional councillor. But commissioners of supply were a numerous species: in 1798 the Stewartry could boast 100 of them. The time required to make longhand copies of the original circular to send to all commissioners would have given Arbigland's favourite son the opportunity to have plundered every seaboard community in Wigtownshire. Is it then possible that the conscientious excise officer feared that Physgill, close to the eastern shore of Luce Bay, might be particularly at risk as the location for an attempted rerun of the previous year's unsuccessful foray to St Mary's Isle, and was he hinting that a prudent, temporary withdrawal to less exposed accommodation might be worth considering?

The removal of any potential threat to the laird of Physgill's wellbeing was his second piece of career good fortune as he almost did not enjoy that status. He had acquired the estate through his wife, Agnes Stewart, but the lady might well not have had such a desirable dowry for in the previous generation her father had been threatened with disinheritance for making a spectacularly unsuitable match in marrying the daughter of "an alehouse keeper".

Sources

Scoular, J.   Hathorn Stewart archive

UNINVITED GUESTS

It is generally believed that in the Second World War Galloway's coasts were spared from the close proximity of German submarines that had characterized the earlier global conflict. A few years ago a Kirkcudbright resident was dramatically made aware of the falseness of this comfortable assumption. He was walking along the cliffs from the Meikle Ross at the head of the Dee estuary to Brighouse Bay when he met an elderly couple, fell into conversation with them, and discovered they hailed from Germany. His conventional, polite enquiry as to whether this was their first visit to the area elicited an unexpected response.

"Oh, no," said the husband with a smile, pointing to Fauldbog Bay below them, "I was here in 1941 when my U-boat was recharging its batteries down there."

The retrospective unease probably created by this anecdote for Galloway residents of the period can only be compounded by a perusal of the catalogue of Luftwaffe aerial reconnaissance photographs of Scotland held by the National Monuments Record of Scotland. This reveals that in three sorties between October, 1940, and January, 1941, the German air force photographed every RAF airfield and flying boat base in Galloway, including the modest grass strip at Kidsdale near Whithorn and the unfinished aerodrome at Baldoon, RAF Wigtown. The fact that the images were probably taken from 30,000 feet seems scant consolation for the intrusion of privacy especially as the flight covering the Wigtown and Stranraer targets took place on the second of January.

Little reassurance is obtained if we seek refuge in the realms of fiction, specifically the works of north-west of England writer Harold Bindloss. Visits to relatives in Wigtown and Garlieston made him familiar with the north shore of the Solway Firth and this familiarity led to *The Laird of Borrans* with its plot based on the Second World War use of that stretch of water and its Galloway hinterland as a conduit for the movement of German spies and saboteurs between their homeland and sensitive areas of the United Kingdom. The urge to dismiss this as risible fiction should perhaps be resisted and not only on topographical and geographical grounds for Bindloss's fiction appears to have a disturbing tendency to mirror events in the real world of which the writer had no knowledge. An earlier book, set and written during the First World War, involved German U-boats refuelling from dumps hidden by agents at remote landing places on the Solway coast of Galloway, a scenario not dissimilar from actual events at Fauldbog Bay in 1941...

<u>Sources</u>

Anon.   personal communication

Bindloss, H.   *Johnstone of the Border*   New York, 1916

Bindloss, H.   *The Laird o' Borrans*   London, 1945

McLaren, K.   *Catalogue of Luftwaffe Photographs in the NMRS*
                        Edinburgh, 1999

FARMING MATTERS

CHILCARROCH: THE PLOUGH AND THE POET

The small, isolated, stock farm of Chilcarroch in the Machars of Wigtownshire north of Mochrum and close to the clachan of Barrachan has unexpected claims to fame on the grounds both of history and of literature, the former claim being the more robust.

The farm has provided the sole surviving example of a vital piece of equipment in the rural economy in the days before the eighteenth century Agricultural Revolution. This was the heavy form of the Old Scots Plough, a formidable implement which required the services of between eight and ten animals to pull it and a team of three to operate it: one man, the gadsman, controlled the animals; one man guided the plough; and the third was responsible for ensuring the plough operated at the correct depth. The draught animals could be oxen, horses, or a combination of the two. Which animal was better for the job was a source of lively and long-running controversy. Supporters of oxen would point to the unarguable fact that when the latter's working days were over they could become a food source, as their rivals could not, at least in this country.

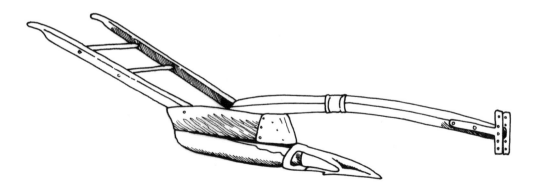

The Chilcarroch plough

Even when the Agricultural Revolution brought lighter ploughs needing fewer draught animals, many farmers kept the Old Scots Plough to break in pasture and work heavy land. The Rev. Samuel Smith, an expert on agriculture in Galloway, says the older plough lasted longest here because it was thought particularly suitable for the stony, broken ground found in many places.

The Chilcarroch example seems to have arrived there in the 1720's or 1730's with the Anderson family, who went on to occupy the farm for over 200 years. They probably brought it with them from nearby Capenoch. After it ceased to be used, it was stored in the rafters of a barn until the 1950's, when it was taken to Stranraer museum, where it now is displayed. Constructed mainly of wood, it has had a handle replaced. This is the result of a youthful member of the Anderson family performing gymnastics by swinging from the plough handles in the barn until one of them broke. The culprit claimed strenuously that the offending handle was badly worm-eaten!

Chilcarroch's literary credentials have been provided by well known Scottish poet Valerie Gillies, chosen in 2005 as Edinburgh's official poet laureate or makar. On a visit to Wigtownshire she was impressed by the way that the farm and steading blend into the landscape because they are built, like many Galloway moorland farms, of local whinstone (greywacke):

"A moorland farm grows out of the hillside.
Where is it hewn stone? Where is it native rock?"

Her poem, *Chilcarroch Farmsteading*, shows not only an awareness of the Andersons' long tenure of the farm but also a welcome if unromantic appreciation of the stern realities of farming life in the less fertile parts of Galloway:

"Inhabited from father to son by men of one occupation,
Whose work waited only for the lark".

Sources

Fenton, A.	*Plough and Spade in Dumfries and Galloway* <u>in</u> *TDGNHAS.* *Vol. XLV* Dumfries, 1968
Fergusson, A.	personal communication
Gillies, V.	*Bed of Stone* Edinburgh, 1984
McColm, S.	personal communication
Wallace, M	personal communication.

SHEEP WITH GOLD TEETH

In his *Large Description of Galloway*, written in 1684, the Episcopalian minister of Kirkinner, Andrew Symson, writing of Glasserton parish near Whithorn, mentioned a remarkable claim. He said he had been told that sheep feeding on the Fell of Barullion (behind Monreith village) often had yellow teeth, that looked as if they had been gilded. Understandably he added sceptically, "I give not much faith to it". Astonishingly a similar claim was made for the same parish nearly 300 years later, in a much less credulous age. In the 1950's the tenant of Glasserton Mains farm just over two miles from the Fell of Barullion related to his banker that many of his sheep had yellow teeth. Those acquainted with the gentleman concerned would be forced to give at least some credence to his statement So was Andrew Symson's seventeenth century scepticism misplaced?

It seems a possible explanation may lie in the presence of iron pyrites (fools' gold) in the ground. Some of the bright, gold-like colour may perhaps leach out into the soil in this area of frequent rainfall. If it does, then it could conceivably stain the teeth of sheep grazing on land where this had occurred for sheep crop the grass very closely.

A similar phenomenon was reported by Symson in the parish of Kirkmaiden on the other side of Luce Bay. Here he stated unreservedly that on the farm of Creechan (south of Drummore) all the sheep had very yellow teeth, adding emphatically "their very skin and wool are yellower than any other sheep in the countrey". And, as at Glasserton, the phenomenon seems to have persisted into the present. Some years ago the farmer at Creechan told a neighbour that his Clydesdale horses had yellow hair on their fetlocks instead of the usual white, a phenomenon which is still visible today. Was this the iron pyrites syndrome again with perhaps an even larger vein of the mineral than at Glasserton?

Symson's comment about the locally unique skin and wool colour of the Creechan sheep is also still true today although the idiosyncratic hue is reddish brown rather than yellow.

Sources

Hannay, A.   personal communication

Hose, Mrs A.   personal communication

Shaw, Mrs L.   personal communication

Symson, A.   *A Large Description of Galloway* Edinburgh, 1823

MUG SHEEP AND SNAP DYKES

In 1777, at the height of the revolution in agriculture, well known authority Andrew Wight was sent by an official government body, The Commissioners of the Annexed Estates, to Galloway to report on the state of agriculture there and suggest what improvements should be made. In the course of his findings, Wight referred to an innovation in sheep farming which had been less than successful. This was the introduction of a new type of sheep from Lincolnshire intended to improve wool yield. The animals were known as mug sheep and the name was unhappily appropriate for they were big with appetites to match, were slow to fatten, and produced meat of poor quality. These disadvantages more than offset any increase in wool yield they could effect and they were soon replaced by other, more euphonious and productive breeds such as Leicesters, Cheviots, and Shetlands. Wight dismissively observed,

"It is a heavy dull creature, not apt to break through fences".

This disinclination of mug sheep to seek greener pastures was not shared by the Blackface sheep, later ubiquitous on the higher grazings of Galloway and notorious for its disregard for field boundaries. In response Galloway dykers developed a special type of structure which Wight calls the snap dyke but which is much better known as the Galloway dyke. Between five and six feet high, this was built double, that is, with two rows of stones and hearting of smaller stones packed in between, to about forty inches high. A row of flat stones was then laid on and the dyke continued for about two feet as a single dyke of biggish, rough stones with wide interstices so that the light shines clearly through. It was claimed with absolute conviction that the latter feature, making the dyke look insecure and liable to collapse easily, is a highly effective deterrent to even the most venturesome Blackface sheep.

Initial reader scepticism about this claim may be tempered by the knowledge that in the early nineteenth century *Survey of Agriculture in Scotland* reporters from no less than seven areas ranging from the Hebrides to Roxburgh mention this special type of dyke, calling it a Galloway- or galloway-dyke. The author of the Argyllshire survey well expresses the consensus:

"The tottering appearance, and seeing light through the stones deter them (the sheep) from any attempt to scale it".

This contention is endorsed by the 1885 *Text book of Farm Engineering*. Those with a persisting credibility problem should seek out such a dyke, still common in upland Galloway, and view it from the vantage point of a Blackface sheep.

Sources

Rainsford-Hannay, F.   *Dry Stone Walling* London, 1957

Wight, A.   *Present State of Husbandry in Scotland, Vol. III*
         Edinburgh, 1777

REMARKABLE RHINNS GATEPILLARS

The stone pillars of field gates understandably do not receive much attention from passers by but some in the Ardwell-Port Logan area of the South Rhinns are well worthy of study. Included in this category are at least two pairs on the minor road leading from Ardwell village to Clachanmore. They are single pieces of worked granite and carved on the front and sides of each pillar is a pattern of linked crosses, which could also be described as forming a vertical series of diamonds or lozenges.

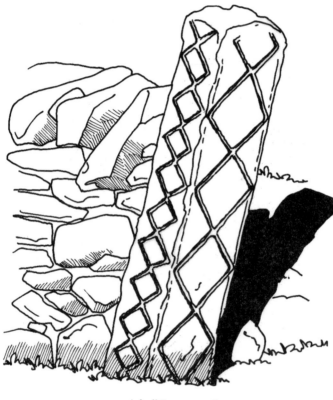

Ardwell Estates gatepillar

Their origin dates to the pre-railway days, when the dominant form of transport linking Galloway to the outside world was by sea and, for long, sailing ship. Geography dictated that Galloway had as a result close links of every kind with Cumbria, as it is now called. Much of the former area's agricultural produce was shipped across the Solway and, in the case of the Southern Rhinns, in some cases ships on the return journey carried those carved stone gate pillars as ballast. The ships involved seem to have been trading for Ardwell Estates as it appears to be only on land owned by them that the pillars are found. Apart from the examples already mentioned in the vicinity of Ardwell church, a single pillar can be seen lying on the ground at the corner of a greenhouse just inside the entrance to the walled garden at Ardwell House. In addition at least one pair can be glimpsed at the roadside on the A75 two miles east of Glenluce close to the entrance to Knockieshea, a property belonging to the Ardwell estate. (Road safety considerations suggest the A75 examples should be taken on trust.)

Surprisingly, the South Rhinns offer another unusual type of gate pillar. This time it is circular and made of roughly dressed, bonded local whinstone. Nothing unusual about that, you may say, but the top of the gate pillar, instead of being flat or rounded, is steeply conical. This seems to be a design characteristic of Ulster, where it is claimed that the conical top is to prevent the Devil sitting on the pillar. Local examples of the type appear to be mainly confined to the South Rhinns, particularly to Logan estate. Several pairs are to be found on the farm of Milhill on the opposite side of the bay from Port Logan village and a single example stands at the roadside on the east side of the B7065 just north of the same village. However, the best place to view the Ulster gate pillar is on the A716 just south of Ardwell village between Chapel Rossan and the entrance to Logan House, where no fewer than eleven examples terminate the parapets of three small bridges, creating an unambiguously Devil-unfriendly location.

The occurrence of an Ulster architectural feature in the South Rhinns is predictable, emphasising the close links over the centuries between the two regions joined by the North Channel. However, the existence of two distinctive types of pillar so close together, with few examples found elsewhere, seems strange and invites speculation. In the nineteenth century a certain rivalry appears to have existed between at least some of the Rhinns estates as regards outward appearances: we may have this to thank for the splendid collections of rhododendrons in which the area abounds. One wonders if in the case of the adjoining Ardwell and Logan estates this rivalry found an expression in field gate pillars. The presence of two columns of the Ulster type lining the main road just over the boundary from Ardwell estate seems more than coincidental.

If competitiveness does lie behind this feature of the South Rhinns landscape, the results are arguably more environmentally beneficial than the current popular form of neighbourly oneupmanship, the Christmas lights display.

Sources

Ulster Architectural Heritage Society   *Historic Buildings in Donaghadee and Portpatrick* Belfast, 1978

Personal communications from former members of the *Discovering Galloway from Books* Stranraer class.

A PERSECUTOR OF PEAT

Scotland's eighteenth century agricultural revolution began earlier in Galloway than anywhere else and lairds like the Earl of Stair at Lochinch and William Craik of Arbigland receive due credit in the histories for their pioneering efforts. However, the work of a twentieth century Galloway agricultural improver languishes largely neglected. And yet travellers on the A75 between Creetown and Newton Stewart have graphic evidence of the success of his methods of land reclamation as they cross the long straight over the Flow of Muirfad. "Flow" is the local word for a peat bog, as the Flow of Muirfad originally was in its entirety. Today only a small central portion remains in that state; most of the Flow is now good pasture on which sheep and cattle profitably graze. The whole provides an excellent "before and after" demonstration of the success of the work of Alex B. Allan, for many years farmer at Muirfad farm at the western (Palnure) end of the Flow.

From 1920 Mr Allan developed a method of transforming peat moss into "one of our richest and most fertile black soils", to use his own words, by liberal application of phosphate, in the form of slag, and lime together with grass and clover seeds. The inferior grasses disappeared and the peat decayed, beginning to change into black soil. For a country like Scotland with its vast areas of peat moss the importance of this technique was great in those times untroubled by concerns about preservation of wild life habitats.

In recognition of his work Alex Allan received the O.B.E. The observant will discover at the roadside in front of his former home at Muirfad a small memorial, usually sadly overgrown. But his real monument is the large numbers of sheep and cattle in the surrounding fields growing fat on the pasture he created.

Sources

Allan, Alex B.   *Peat into Pasture* in *Scottish Forestry* Edinburgh(?), 19--
Hare, F.K.   *The Land* of *Britain: Kirkcudbright and Wigtown*   London,
                       1942

HOW THE BELTIE GOT ITS BELT

As the emblem of its native province the Belted Galloway has reached iconic status, and its myriad representations in an astonishing variety of media are a tribute to local commercial ingenuity. Sadly an investigation into the origins of its remarkable colouring takes us far from the imaginative creations of Rudyard Kipling's *Just So Stories* into the complex, prosaic world of animal genetics.

However, before we take that step it is worth acknowledging the contribution to the debate of the Rev. Samuel Clanaghan of Glasserton in 1838, one which would surely have earned the amused respect of Kipling. Writing in the *New Statistical Account* and dealing with local agriculture, the minister darkly commented, "Some believe…that the very sight of Ayrshire cows in the neighbourhood corrupts the native breed, and that it often causes Galloways of the purest breed, and blackest colour, to produce red, speckled, and spotted calves", from which it seems but a short step to belts.

Back in the sternly logical world of science, Dutch researchers have claimed that the famous white belt is the result of a loss of pigment due to inadequate functioning of ganglion cells in the sympathetic nervous system for these control nutrition and circulation. Since this deficiency is caused by a gene, selective breeding will produce animals with the desired belts, although the width of the belt will be variable, depending on the number of inadequately functioning cells. Perhaps we should stick with the Rev. Clanaghan…

Shaken by the revelation that the famous colour scheme is the result of a physiological flaw, the local enthusiast will take no comfort from the fact that, far from our local heroes being unique, belted cattle were recorded in ninth century Bohemia in what is now the Czech Republic and that today they graze happily

Detail from 15th century Austrian painting

in locations as diverse as Wales, Switzerland, and Mongolia. In fact, it may be that Belted Galloways originate in a cross between imported Dutch belted cattle and the local, monotone breed.

As most local art exhibitions will testify, belted cattle exert a powerful attraction on artists and have done from as early as the fifteenth century, when they feature in an Austrian painting, to the present and the work of celebrated Scottish practitioner James Macintosh Patrick. Mainly a landscape painter, Macintosh Patrick was commissioned in 1958 by Lord David Stuart of Old Place of Mochrum to capture on canvas a prize-winning cow. Perhaps understandably, the artist found the task a difficult one as the animal inconveniently refused to stand still, being concerned about the wellbeing of her new calf. Doubtless the painter returned to his native Dundee and subjects like the more amenable Tay rail bridge with some relief.

Sources

Crighton, M.   personal communication
Stuart, Lord D.   *An Illustrated History of Belted Cattle* Edinburgh, 1970
_____   *The (New) Statistical Account of Wigtonshire*
                          Edinburgh, 1841

INDUSTRIES

TATTIE MILLS

Galloway has never been an area noted for manufacturing industry. Any activity of this kind has been usually small-scale and has involved the processing of agricultural products. Some of those manufactures, such as cheesemaking, textiles, and tanning, are well documented but less well recorded is the industry of potato processing. The story of one mill, the complex at Fordbank between Wigtown and Bladnoch, perhaps encapsulates the history of the industry in Galloway. Its chequered story is fairly typical of all its kind and at different times it manufactured virtually every product that can be obtained from potatoes.

All that survived of Fordbank tattie mill in 2006 (millwheel conjectural)

The Fordbank mill was established in 1832 by John McClelland, a member of a well known local family of farmers, two of whom had founded the Bladnoch distillery fifteen years before; it seems likely that links between distillery and potato mill were always close. The new enterprise does not seem to have prospered for it was offered for sale (as a potato flour mill) three years later. In fact it stayed in the McClelland family but experienced rapid changes of use, being described in 1850 as a "starch manufactory": starch from potatoes is used for a variety of industrial purposes. Two years later it is listed as "a manufactory for farina" (potato flour or meal). The reason for the latter change of use was almost certainly the notorious Potato Blight of 1850, best known for its effects in Ireland. A *Wigtown Free Press* report of October, 1850,disconcertingly relates that farmers are able to obtain a fair price for diseased potatoes by sending them for processing to Wigtownshire's five farina mills, all of which are consequently "busy grinding potatoes". This episode emphasises how the industry was always heavily affected by national and international events, inevitable perhaps with a product of limited appeal.

The mid-nineteenth century appears to have been one of the industry's peaks: in 1863 Fordbank is described as an "extensive preserved potatoe manufactory and farina mill". Despite its spelling, the quotation indicates that the mill is now manufacturing two different products: potato flour and preserved potatoes. A comparison of Ordnance Survey maps of the period shows the adjective "extensive" to be justified for at this time the mill was substantially enlarged. The machinery was also now steam-powered whereas Fordbank had originally relied on water power from the Trammonford burn with a holding dam near the present football field.Yet by 1890 the notoriously volatile industry seems to have been in recession again for in that year the McClellands attempted a remarkable new diversification for their ailing mill: wine production. In continental Europe, particularly Germany, the production of alcohol by the fermentation of a cooked mass of potatoes using yeast followed by distillation is common but not so in Britain and the method is not associated with the production of wine.

However, evidence for this unlikely change of course is found in a booklet published by George McClelland in 1890 and appropriately titled *Wine Wonders in Wigtownshire*. From this source we learn with some surprise that after many years' experiment Mr McClelland is now producing a cornucopia of delights: champagne, port, sherry, and burgundy while testimonials from satisfied customers all over Britain confirm the high quality of the Fordbank vintages. Unfortunately no independent documentary evidence of Mr McClelland's enterprise has been found but local recollection confirms that wine was indeed produced at the mill. A Wigtown resident remembers that when he was a boy some of his peers sneaked into the complex after its closure in the 1920's and reported that wine was stored there.Thirty years later, in 1957, some locals, digging in the rubble of the now demolished mill, uncovered a quantity of bottled wine in what had been a cellar. The wine was drunk and enjoyed by several local people.

Mr McClelland could have produced his range of wines in various ways, some involving potato spirit or yeast from the nearby distillery owned by the same family. Perhaps the most likely possibility is that he used the methods of the modern home wine maker, importing grape pulp and fermenting it himself, adding the other necessary ingredients. It is unlikely that Machars vineyards produced much of his raw material. His enterprise does not appear to have caused any major competition problems for importers of traditional wines.

A more significant boost to Fordbank's fortunes was provided by the First World War, which created a substantial demand for its then products, tinned potatoes and probably also potato flour. A considerable number of local women were employed there and a burgh resident recalled following a load of flour to Wigtown harbour, where it was loaded on a ship supposedly for troops on the Western Front. However, demand dropped with the end of hostilities and the mill finally closed in the early 1920's. In 1940 the buildings were sold to Wigtown Town Council, by whom they were first partly and then totally demolished. Later private houses were built on part of the site. Today the only trace of this century-old industrial enterprise is a low pile of vegetation-covered rubble between the boundary wall of Fordbank Hotel and the first modern bungalow, together with the stone-built garage, now converted into a house, immediately adjacent within the hotel grounds. An 1850 map indicates that the garage was originally part of the mill buildings.

The demise of Fordbank and the other Galloway potato mills was probably the result of decreased demand after the end of the First World War. Demand for their products was always very variable, being at its lowest under normal circumstances for dried or processed potatoes were not a popular food. In wartime the mills prospered for the armed services provided a large and (officially) uncomplaining market. In general, for the potato processing sector bad times were good times. Another problem for the industry was its highly competitive nature: in Wigtownshire alone six mills (at Fordbank, at Newmilns just west of Wigtown, at Minnigaff, at Elrig, and at two sites in Stranraer) struggled for the patronage of a reluctant market. Today evidence of the existence of this small but interesting contribution to the local economy is, as the Fordbank example shows, difficult to find on the ground but surely worth the effort: a bottle of local champagne might well be the reward!

Sources

Campbell, R.	personal communication
Fraser, G.	*Sketches and Anecdotes of the Royal Burgh of Wigtown* Wigtown, 1864
Gardiner, G.	personal communication
Irving, D.	personal communication
Nicol, D.	personal communication

Nicol, J.   personal communication
Redcliffe, S.   *The History and Social Influences of the Potato*
Ordnance Survey   various maps
Stewart, Ms. M.   material from Dumfries and Galloway Council archives
                                   Wigtownshire Free Press various issues

TREACLE WORKS

In the Machars of Wigtownshire until recent times a traditional condemnation of a lazy or incompetent manual worker was that he should be sent to Sorbie to tramp treacle at the treacle works there. In some versions the treacle was to be tramped into bottles and in others hobnailed boots were to be worn. A few years ago a possible explanation for this strange saying emerged. Apparently in South-West England, where mining for various minerals was formerly carried on, references to treacle mining were a common form of humour in local speech. It has been suggested that if similar references are found in Scotland it shows the existence in the area in question of Cornish lead miners, many of whom came to Scotland in the nineteenth century. On Tonderghie estate near Isle of Whithorn the Mary Mine, which produced small quantities of lead and copper, has been worked on three different occasions, one of them in the nineteenth century.

It seems conceivable that the local expression is a version of the traditional Cornish joke brought to the area by natives of that county working at the Mary Mine. The reason for the choice of Sorbie as location for the mythical industry may be that for the Cornish miners at Tonderghie Sorbie was known by name only and represented an Ultima Thule, a location on the edge of the known world.

The joke is also found in the Stewartry attached to the village of Palnackie on the Urr Water. A well known local resident suggested that the source was the fact that barrels of treacle were often shipped from Liverpool to Palnackie, frequently arriving holed so that the vessels' decks were covered with treacle. However various mine workings were located a few miles from Palnackie in the vicinity of Auchencairn and in the mid-nineteenth century English miners were resident in the latter village. It seems possible therefore that the mythical Palnackie treacle works had exactly the same Cornish origins as its Wigtownshire counterpart.

Sources

Halliday, G.	*Palnackie* Dalbeattie, 1993
Macleod, I.	*Discovering Galloway* Edinburgh, 1986
Maxwell, G.	personal communication
Vance, Mrs. C.	personal communication

THE WHITHORN MAN WHO CO-FOUNDED ESSO

Most people have heard of John D. Rockefeller, the archetypal American business millionaire, but few know about the Wigtownshire man who was one of his business partners in the creation of perhaps the world's best known oil company.

Charles Lockhart was born in 1818 on the farm of Cairnhead between Whithorn and Isle of Whithorn on the shores of Wigtown Bay. His father was tenant of Cairnhead but when Charles left school at 14 he did not go on to the farm. Instead he found employment in his great uncle's general store in nearby Garlieston. His entrepreneurial spirit soon manifested itself for after two years he opened his own grocer's business in Isle of Whithorn. But two years later another career change occurred when he joined the rest of his family in emigrating to the United States. Their destination was Ohio, where father Lockhart intended to farm, but when they reached Pittsburgh young Charles "thought I had been idle long enough" and left the others to find employment in James McCully's large wholesale and retail grocery business. He was soon promoted but at the same time pursued one or two ventures on his own account.

In 1852 he became involved almost by accident in the birth of the American oil industry when he became part-owner of a salt-producing well which also yielded some petroleum. Previously petroleum had been used only for medicinal purposes but a method had just been discovered of distilling kerosene (paraffin) from mineral oil to burn in lamps and demand for petroleum had soared. Lockhart saw the opportunity and his company leased land and started drilling successfully for oil. It also moved into oil refining and in 1860 Lockhart came back to Britain to negotiate the deal which brought the first US oil to this country.

However, in 1874, with the age of the internal combustion engine not yet dawned, the infant oil industry was suffering from over-production. It was then that Lockhart, joint owner of the biggest group of refineries in Pittsburgh, was approached by John D. Rockefeller, owner of the biggest refining company in Cleveland. The result was that the two groups of companies, together with the biggest firm in Philadelphia, merged into a single company called the Standard Oil Company, the name coming from one of Lockhart's companies. The new combine's name was soon shortened to Esso and the rest is history… Lockhart continued to run the Pittsburgh end of Esso's business until 1890, when at the age of 72 he ended his active involvement in the oil industry which he had helped to found and which had made him a millionaire and ensured his place in American business history.

However, the oil mogul did not forget his Wigtownshire ties, strengthened by his marriage to a girl from the farm of High Skeog just outside Whithorn. Around 1890 he bought the mansion of Dildawn just west of Castle Douglas on the banks of the Dee and clearly visible from the A75. It was intended as a free timeshare for the use of his wife's relatives but for some reason he sold the house ten years later and so the Walkers lost their holiday destination. After his death in 1905 his son sought to redress what he felt was this shabby treatment of his mother's family. He therefore set up a trust fund to provide them and after their deaths their spouses and children with a monthly income totalling £1,000 a year. Modest by today's standards, this sum represented undreamed of wealth in early and mid-twentieth century Wigtownshire. Thus were created the famous "£20-a-week Walkers", part of local folk lore. It is likely that none of this exclusive club now survives but in an era when oil seems to dominate not only the world economy but world politics as well it is worth remembering that one of the industry's founders was a farmer's son from outside Whithorn.

Sources

Anon.   *Charles Lockhart* (from in-house magazine?)
Lawrie, T.   personal communication
Walker A.   personal communication

GALLOWAY'S SOUTH SEA BUBBLE

The South Sea Bubble financial scandal, which rocked the national economy in the early eighteenth century, is a celebrated event but less well known is another financial scandal 50 years later with strong Galloway connections. Yet no less a person than Dr Samuel Johnson declared the second event to be comparable to the earlier one as a cause of "extensive distress and...frightful alarm." And the great Scottish economist Adam Smith devoted part of his classic *The Wealth of Nations* to an analysis of the causes of the affair.

The institution which caused all this furore was the Douglas, Heron and Company bank established at Ayr in 1769 and hence often known as the Ayr Bank. Of its two founders the Hon. Archibald Douglas of Douglas fortunately had no Galloway connections but Patrick Heron, laird of Kirroughtree just outside Newton Stewart, obviously had. At a time when the burgeoning Scottish economy was constrained by a lack of capital, the Ayr bank was intended to remedy that deficiency. Many of the most prominent landowners in south-west Scotland were among the 140 eager subscribers to the new enterprise. The bank's liberal policy of letting "no one depart empty-handed" ensured a flow of customers. However loan applications were subject to less than rigorous examination so that, in the words of a contemporary, money was advanced for "foolish, ill conducted, and unsuccessful speculations". Many of those loans were to directors: at one time advances of this type amounted to £400,000. It did not help that none of the directors had any experience of banking so that too much was left to officials often incompetent or dishonest. The same contemporary described the Ayr bank's operations as "a train of knavery, folly, and mismanagement". The incipient disaster was accelerated by the bank's three branches, at Ayr, Dumfries, and Edinburgh, having equal status but operating in complete independence of one another.

The inevitable crash came in 1772, when the firm ceased trading, going into liquidation in 1773. Loans previously obtained from other banks in a vain attempt to redress the situation meant that the company had heavy debts. The shareholders, who had lost their own investments, had to repay those debts with the result that by 1775 half of them had become insolvent and estates that had been in the possession of a family for generations had to be sold. In a grim version of the game of Last Man Standing a decreasing number of shareholders shouldered the company's outstanding debts. The latter were eventually paid in full but the final loss to shareholders was over £600,000 and many well known families disappeared from the Galloway landholding scene.

And what of Patrick Heron of Kirroughtree, joint author of the ill starred enterprise? He too experienced major financial difficulties and for a time had to vacate his splendid mansion, built around 1720 and today a hotel. Tradition says he took up quarters in a modest dwelling close to its east lodge. It has been suggested that this may have been "Heroncroft", the house that stands back from the road at the west end of Blackcraig village. From here he proceeded to restore the family fortunes by successful involvement in the risky cattle droving business: a major droving route bifurcated near his front door. By 1793 he was back in his mansion, where he entertained Robert Burns on the latter's visit to Galloway. To complete a remarkable rehabilitation he stood successfully the following year for the Stewartry of Kirkcudbright parliamentary seat, gaining election in those pre-reform days on the votes of the landed proprietors, many of whom had suffered severe financial loss twenty years before from the collapse of the bank he had founded. Further proof of Heron's remarkable ability to induce amnesia is that Burns's companion on his Kirroughtree visit was John Syme, who was apparently happy to accept the laird's hospitality although his father had been ruined by the collapse of the Ayr Bank.

Sources

Brady, F.	*So Fast to Ruin* Ayr, 1973
Campbell, R. H.	*Scotland Since 1707: The Rise of an Industrial Society* Oxford, 1965
Heron, R.	*Observations Made in a Journey Through the Western Counties of Scotland* Perth, 1793
Russell, J.A.	*The Book of Galloway* Dumfries, 1962
Wilson, Mrs. C.	personal communication

AN EARLY WIGTOWNSHIRE AGRICULTURAL COLLEGE

The traveller on the glorious moorland road that runs from near Kirkcowan south-west by way of Mochrum lochs to Culshabbin may wonder about the large house known as Craigeach which stands halfway along that road on its east side. Its size and its construction of dressed whinstone with sandstone window- and door surrounds together with its crow-stepped gables suggest this is no ordinary farmhouse. That impression is reinforced by the absence of any obvious steading and by clumps of rhododendron ponticum where the drive leaves the public road. In fact, Craigeach is, or was, one of the more unusual educational institutions in a Galloway not devoid of such phenomena.

Craigeach

It was built in 1890, as a plaque on the front of the building testifies, and the prime mover behind its creation seems to have been the third Marchioness of Bute, who had a keen interest in social welfare. She apparently persuaded her husband, who owned nearby Old Place of Mochrum and the Mochrum Loch estate, to set up in this lonely spot a purpose-built agricultural training centre for orphan boys. Presumably the practical side of the course was carried out on the estate home farm nearby or utilising the small steading which stands unobtrusively behind the house. Although the first director, Donald Robertson, may have been a layman, the school seems to have been run for most of its existence by Roman Catholic priests. The name longest associated with it was that of Irish-born Father Vignoles (or Vignoeles), described in one source as Director, Craigeach Training Centre for Orphan Boys, and someone with close links with the Bute family. He combined his Craigeach duties with those of local parish priest, as presumably did another director, Father Thomas Joyce, during his tenure from 1898 to 1900. However, Craigeach did not survive long into the new century, closing down around 1907, perhaps after the death of the moving spirit behind it, the Marchioness of Bute.

Several recollections of the school survive, suggesting that it had a substantial impact on the local population. It seems to have been known locally as "The Reformatory" and its occupants were believed to be boys who had been in trouble. A local resident remembers going on holiday to relatives at nearby May farm as a small boy and, even though the school had closed, being warned that if he misbehaved he would be sent to Craigeach to the "bad boys' school". A former inhabitant of the area told how in his early years he was occasionally sent on errands to Craigeach and came away as fast as possible because he was apprehensive of the boys there. And local recollection confirms that the school catered for orphans: a Newton Stewart man remembers a rag-and-bone merchant, long deceased, in the town by the name of David McMeikan. David was both an orphan and a former pupil of Craigeach. The school had clearly given him standards of social behaviour for even though he lived alone he always donned a collar and tie for dinner.

Oral reminiscences also furnish details of the physical accommodation at the school. In addition to the main building one or more auxiliary buildings may have been used. A former estate worker says a lean-to, corrugated-iron building formerly stood at the back of the house and had been used to teach the boys boot-mending. Seemingly local people brought their footwear there to have repairs done. A second, small, free-standing structure of similar construction stood on the site; it has been suggested that it was used either as a chapel or as an extra classroom. Some time after the school closed this building was bought by a Port William resident, Mr Tom Drysdale, and re-erected as a bungalow on Monreith shore, where it still stands but in much altered form.

Craigeach's useful life continued after its closure as an educational establishment As early as 1908 it seems to have been converted into accommodation for estate workers and their families, being split into three "flats". The farm manager, the forester, and a shepherd are all recorded as having lived there. This second chapter in Craigeach's history lasted until at least 1972. And the house still stands in solitary state today as a monument to a pious lady's desire to aid the lot of her fellow human beings.

Sources

Brown, G.   personal communication

Brown, M.   personal communication

Hume, John   *Dumfries and Galloway; An Illustrated Archtectural Guide*
                                 Edinburgh, 2000

MacCaig, W.   personal communication

McFadzean, S.   personal communication

Maxwell, J.   personal communication

Miller, D.   personal communication

Wallace, M.   personal communication

Watt, J. Innes   *The Roman Catholic Church in Mochrum* <u>in</u> *Mochrum…*
                                 A Parish History Wigtown, 1994

Wigtown County Council   valuation rolls

THE TALENTED DOUGLAS FAMILY

The entrepreneurial achievements of Sir William Douglas of Newton Douglas (later Newton Stewart), Castle Douglas, and Gelston Castle have led to other members of that remarkable family receiving less attention than they merit. Yet it must be remembered that Sir William did not operate on his own but as part of the family import-export business between Britain and her American colonies. His brother George was also in the business and the fact that it survived the War of Independence and went on to flourish again perhaps owes not a little to George. When war broke out in 1776, the latter, who had settled in New York, threw in his lot with the colonists. It is not impossible that his decision was for commercial rather than political reasons, ensuring that the family firm prudently backed both sides. Perhaps significantly, his brother-in-law kept a portrait of the ousted king, George III, hidden in the cellar of his New York home and would take his grandchildren down to view it with the injunction,

"Bow to your master!"

Whatever the reason for George's choice, it proved a profitable one not only for the firm but for the gentleman's family. They went on to become leading members of New York society and to be related to three American presidents: James Monroe, Theodore Roosevelt, and Franklin D. Roosevelt.

Another participant in the family import-export business was almost certainly Sir William's first cousin Samuel. Samuel like George settled in America, being variously a merchant in Georgia and owner of a tea and coffee plantation in Jamaica before dying in South Carolina in 1799. The expatriate's love for his native soil revealed itself in his final dispositions. He instructed that his body, placed in a lead coffin, was to be returned to Scotland for interment in Newton Stewart, principal settlement of Penninghame parish, in which his mother and father had been born. Regrettably it took three years for this instruction to be

Sir William Douglas's mausoleum at Kelton outside Castle Douglas.

carried out (the implications are best not considered). A similar delay attended the implementation of his other gesture to his home area, the creation of a free school for indigent children in either Penninghame parish or neighbouring Kirkmabreck, the parish of his birth. Even the appointment of "my first cousin and much loved friend William Douglas" as a trustee failed to expedite matters. It was 31 years before the school at the north end of Newton Stewart was built and opened. It became known as the Douglas Academy and in 1922 combined with the Ewart High School to create the Douglas-Ewart High School, which still provides secondary education for the Machars of Wigtownshire.

A third member of the Douglas family deserving of a higher profile is William, nephew of Sir William and son of James of Orchardton, the latter reputedly an abler businessman than his more famous brother. Unlike his already mentioned relatives William did not enter the commercial world. A brilliant scholar, perhaps helped by having "shepherd boy to professor" Alexander Murray as his tutor, he attended Cambridge University before becoming an Edinburgh advocate and then an MP. He was also a good artist, arguably unsurprising in view of a distant relationship with the famous Faed family of Gatehouse. Proof of his artistic talents can still be found in the Castle Douglas area in the form of his uncle's mausoleum at Kelton, which William designed. Its striking mix of Greek, Egyptian, and Oriental features might incline the passing visitor to believe that Glasgow's Alexander "Greek" Thomson had spent a working vacation in the area.

The continental holidays which probably provided the inspiration for those exotic architectural features also tragically led to William's death. Having suffered severe sunstroke in Greece, he received inappropriate treatment and never recovered, dying at home at Orchardton at the age of 37, mourned not only for his intellectual and artistic gifts but for his generosity of spirit. This exhibited itself in the financial support and assistance he gave Alexander Murray, his erstwhile tutor, and famously in an incident involving a local tramp. The latter was leaving Orchardton House when he encountered young William Douglas. Asked why he looked so disconsolate, he explained that he had asked William's mother for an old pair of trousers to replace the barely respectable ones he was wearing but had been peremptorily refused.

"Change trousers with me," said the resourceful son of the house. "My mother won't refuse to give me another pair."

Sources

Alsop, J. and S. *Lament for a Long-Gone Past* in the *Saturday Evening Post*, Jan., 26th, 1957 New York, 1957

Duncan, N. personal communication

McLay, J. D. *The Douglas-Ewart High School* Dumfries, 1994

Trotter, A. *East Galloway Sketches* Castle Douglas, 1901

"GOLD IN THEM THAR HILLS"

The Wanlockhead area in the Lowther Hills has been famous for hundreds of years as a source of gold, enjoying the appellation "God's Treasure House in Scotland". Less well known is the fact that the Carsphairn locality, twenty miles to the west, is also associated with that desirable commodity. The claim is made by the parish minister in 1839 in the *New Statistical Account*. He relates the remarkable tale of a Mr Dodds who "in former times" obtained alluvial gold from streams running off Cairnsmore of Carsphairn, "the highest of the three" hills in Galloway bearing the name Cairnsmore. The gold was used to mint coins in a foreign currency but the enterprising prospector fell foul of a 1424 act of parliament reserving all gold found in Scotland to the crown, the foreign currency stratagem obviously having failed. Prior to his arrest a frustrated Mr Dodds threw his coin dies into the evocatively named Green Well of Scotland just north of Carsphairn. The story was repeated by Harper in his *Rambles in Gallloway* and in Trotter's *Galloway Gossip; The Stewartry* with some additional details in both cases.

These details fleshed out the account considerably. Dodds became a doctor (presumably because of his metallurgical skills) and a German living in the reign of King James VI. Alluvial gold was unusually obtained by him from near the headwaters of burns by using miniature mill- or water wheels, the blades of which were coated with a mercurial ointment. The good doctor stirred up the sediment at the bottom of the burn with a spade and when the muddy water ran through the mills the grains of gold adhered to the blades. At the end of the day the material removed from the blades was processed in a workshop still on the lands of Lagwine and the gold separated from the mercury ointment to be minted into Spanish doubloons. Details were furnished of the doctor's fate: trial at Edinburgh and banishment.

The cautionary tale of Dr Dodds must have been well known in Galloway for Mrs Maria Trotter in *Galloway Gossip* recalls that as a child she with her friends made miniature mill wheels of rushes or wood to play with in burns and called them "Dr Dodds's mills". Mrs Trotter was born and brought up in Penninghame parish a substantial distance from Carsphairn; one wonders if the reminiscence in fact originated from her Glenkens-born husband.

The story raises tantalising questions because of possible links with the Wanlockhead area just twenty miles away as the crow flies. Both locations are associated with lead- and gold mining. Dr Dodds is described as a German: mining at Wanlockhead in the sixteenth century was carried on by German miners. The doctor's name may be significant: Dodds is clearly not a German name but Wanlockhead is closely surrounded by hills bearing the name "Dod": Wanlock Dod, Sowen Dod, White Dod. Other Dods occur in the vicinity. And in a 1907 postcard the name of the first hill is spelled "Dodd". A definite connection exists between the two areas for when Col. Cathcart opened the Woodhead lead mine at Carsphairn in 1838 he obtained the bulk of his workforce from Wanlockhead and Leadhills.

It may not be inconceivable that the slightly improbable tale of Mr Dodds and his foreign coin dies was a humorous creation of the Woodhead miners taken at face value by the compiler of the *New Statistical Account* entry for Carsphairn parish to become, with the usual embellishments, a part of local folklore. However, it has to be conceded that this speculation is somewhat suspect on chronological grounds: in defiance of tabloid rules of practice the facts do slightly get in the way of a good story. Alternatively the 1839 *NSA* account may be based on a local folk tradition arising from a German or Dutch miner coming over the hills from Wanlockead in the sixteenth century to prospect for alluvial gold in the Carsphairn area, the prosaic facts having been comprehensively confused and enhanced in the intervening centuries.

The story interestingly in its fully developed form contains some surprisingly precise facts about the technology of gold extraction. Mercury is indeed used in obtaining gold from ore or sediment as it absorbs the gold, the two being later separated by distillation. Water wheels or paddles for one purpose or another play a part in gold mining. Even the time of the story is close to historical fact: German miners were in the area not in the reign of James VI but certainly in that of James V. Whatever questions and contradictions remain (and there are many) the ingenious Dodds and his enterprise surely belong to fact-based legend and not to fiction. And it may be that his "Spanish doubloons" give us Scotland's first example of money laundering…

Sources

Donnachie, I.	*Industrial Archaeology of Galloway*	Newton Abbot, 1971
Harper, M.	*Rambles in Galloway*	Dalbeattie, 1896
Hunter, Mrs. S.	personal communication	
Pickin, J.	personal communication	
Trotter, R. de B.	*Galloway Gossip; The Stewartry* (Dumfries, 1901)	
Wanlockhead Museum Trust	*All About Wanlockhead*	Wanlockhead, 1989
----------	*The New Statistical Account of Scotland*	Edinburgh, 1895

TRANSPORT

LONELY LOCH SKERROW

Of all the stations on the old Dumfries-Stranraer railway, arguably the best known was also the smallest, Loch Skerrow on the shores of the loch of that name in the almost trackless and uninhabited heart of Galloway between New Galloway and Gatehouse stations, "one of the most desert tracts of moorland in Scotland". It was the very remoteness of the halt that impressed it on travellers' memory. Despite its isolation the location played a humble part in the Galloway economy even before the railway came for its sand was collected for sharpening scythes and pearl fishing carried on in its waters.

Loch Skerrow station

When work on the railway line began in 1858 a camp of wooden huts for navvies was built at the north end of the loch but originally no station was planned here. However, shortly after the line opened a water tank was built for the refreshment of thirsty engines after the long 1 in 80 climb up from Loch Ken and New Galloway station. Eventually a passing loop was added and a tiny colony of houses built for the platelayers and signalmen stationed here. For their convenience short wooden platforms were added but until 1955 this was not an official stopping place. Nevertheless trains did stop for the loch was popular with anglers, being stocked with trout and in the care of an angling association. Professor Charles McNeil recollected spending a fortnight's fishing holiday there in 1919, enjoying the simple comfort of one of the railwaymen's cottages. And in December, 1875, presumably by arrangement, 200 curlers accompanied by their supporters alighted at Loch Skerrow to play the Grand Rhins-Machars Curling Match of 50 rinks on the frozen loch.

Augmenting their pay by providing food and sometimes acting as boatmen for visiting fishermen was one of the compensations for railwaymen at this lonely posting. (Provision of accommodation was unusual: Professor McNeil was brother-in-law of the railway company manager.) A remote-area allowance of one shilling a week, paid from 1908, together with six tons of free coal annually, was another. And railwaymen or members of their families could travel free to Castle Douglas once a week to obtain provisions. But there were formidable drawbacks. While railwaymen's children at Gatehouse (Dromore) station travelled free daily to attend school at Mossdale close to New Galloway station, until 1912 trains did not stop at Loch Skerrow for the same purpose. Consequently children of primary school age were taught by their mothers while those of secondary age lodged at Castle Douglas during the week to attend school there. And the halt's isolation and loneliness are emphasised by its use as a rehabilitation posting for staff who had transgressed in some way. On the other hand in the early twentieth century Alexander Cowan served, apparently by choice, for eighteen years as senior signalman at Loch Skerrow.

Despite its remoteness the station was brushed by the Two World Wars. In 1916 off-duty railway employees came to collect sphagnum moss from the surrounding moorland for processing and use in medical dressings while a short distance to the west and close to the railway track stands an unusual monument to a World War Two Polish squadron pilot whose Hawker Typhoon fighter crashed there. It consists of parts of the aircraft's engine cemented to the top of a boulder. The pilot was en route with his squadron, No. 440, from Prestwick to an airfield in Kent to take part in the operation to shoot down the German V1 flying bombs which were being launched against London.

The continuing fascination of Loch Skerrow is shown by its use as the location of a short story *The Green Man* by well known writer and former Stewartry resident Margaret Elphinstone. The plot, involving an encounter between an extra-terrestrial alien of vivid green hue encamped near the old station and a local art teacher walking the line from Mossdale to Gatehouse, seems to strain credulity but the combination of the author's detailed, local, topographical knowledge and her vivid descriptions makes the story disturbingly believable. Since at least one of the railwaymen sent in the past to Loch Skerrow for rehabilitation had been guilty of indulging in alcoholic refreshment while on duty, it may be that Margaret Elphinstone's Green Man was not the first to have been seen at Loch Skerrow.

Sources

Fryer, C.   *The Portpatrick and Wigtownshire Railways* Oxford, 1991
McNeil, C.   *Auld Lang Syne in the Rhins of Galloway* Stranraer, 1956
Smith, D.   *The Little Railways of South-West Scotland* Newton
                     Abbot, 1969
Starling, P.   *Monuments and Moorlands* Stranraer, 1993
Thorne, H.D.   *Rails to Portpatrick* Prescot, 1976

BRIDGING THE KEN

For long the Ken-Dee river system constituted a serious obstacle to east-west communications. This was especially so at New Galloway, where it was crossed by the highway from Edinburgh to Wigtown and Whithorn, the Old Edinburgh Road. Even when the Reformation ended the route's status as the premier pilgrim way in Scotland, it was still a vital artery linking the capital with the two royal burghs of the Machars. The crossing in the vicinity of New Galloway was originally by fords or ferry close to the present bridge but these were unreliable as the local minister noted in 1793:

"A bridge over the Ken at New Galloway would be a great improvement as the crossing is often impassable by ford or ferry boat."

In fact moves to build such a bridge had begun 40 years before for in 1752 the commissioners of supply, local lairds who were the forerunners of the county council, agreed to build a bridge at New Galloway as soon as funds permitted (shades of today). That decision started a cycle of plans-estimates-contract-construction-destruction which was to last for over sixty years and saw at least four structures rise and fall. The culprit was in every case the rowdy River Ken, which, according to our 1793 informant, could rise seven feet when in spate.

The commissioners could not be faulted for failure to explore every option: bridges of wood, iron, and stone were either suggested or built. The solution was eventually found by enlisting Glenkens stone to fight Glenkens water for the present bridge is built of granite from Bennane Hill south of New Galloway. Actual and estimated costs varied widely, evidence presumably that inflation is not a modern phenomenon. At the lower end of the scale Viscount Kenmure's replacement wooden bridge of 1754 was built for a modest £50 while a proposed iron version of 1813 had an estimated price tag of £6715.

As with materials so with civil engineers; the commissioners spread their net widely. Mr John Paterson of Leith, who produced an early nineteenth century design, may not be a household name but Thomas Telford and John Rennie certainly are. In spite of being the greatest civil engineer of the time Telford had an unhappy relationship with the Ken Bridge project. Plans he submitted in 1811 were rejected by the Treasury, now providing a grant for the structure, as being "objectionable because of the excessive curvature". The commissioners further lacerated Telford's professional pride the following year by asking his great rival and fellow Scotsman John Rennie to produce a design for a bridge. The final blow was administered in 1813 when the same body sent Telford the plans of Rennie's newly completed Cree Bridge at Newton Stewart with an

Enquiry whether a similar bridge would be suitable for New Galloway. The great man's reply (if any!) is sadly not recorded.

It was John Rennie who eventually conquered the turbulent waters of the Ken with his bridge of 1820-21, adopting several stratagems for taming the river. His design overleaps not only the watercourse but its flood plain to the west. His five large arches (the central one with a span of ninety feet) are designed to ensure minimum impediment to the free flow of water. For further insurance he altered the river bed, presumably by deepening the channel. An additional reason for the very large central arch may have been the theoretical possibility of the revival of the Glenkens canal scheme, abandoned twenty years before. This would have provided a waterway from the sea at Kirkcudbright via Loch Ken to "the boat- pool at Dalry". Rennie's bridge is a model of good design: it has performed its job efficiently for over 180 years while its elegant lines, best appreciated from a distance and an elevation, enhance the attractiveness of the valley at that point.

We do not have the name of the actual builder of Rennie's bridge but we do know the identities of some of his predecessors who toiled in vain over the years. In 1804 Samuel M'Kean was awarded a sum not to exceed £133 for work on the bridge of the day over and above the contractual agreement (surely evidence of unforeseen problems in the construction). And in 1815 after a partly built stone bridge (perhaps John Rennie's first attempt) had been swept away "by a great flood", contractor Joseph Simpson died, leaving the commissioners with a ruined edifice on which they had spent £2,500. They, like many of their predecessors, might well have echoed with necessary alteration Queen Mary Tudor's famous words about Calais and declared that post-mortem dissection would reveal the words "Ken Bridge" lying in their hearts.

And so today's travellers easing effortlessly across the River Ken below New Galloway would do well to remember the toil, tears, sweat, and blasted hopes that lie behind their easy passage.

But New Galloway might well not have been the site of the bridge that eventually overcame the Ken-Dee obstacle for other candidates were seriously considered. In 1811, the year Telford's plans for a single-span metal bridge with stone abutments near New Galloway were rejected apparently for aesthetic reasons, Rennie submitted drawings for a similarly constructed bridge at Boat of Rhone at an eye-watering cost of over fourteen thousand pounds. Worryingly his plans show the width of the loch at this narrow point as 180 feet whereas the railway engineers who built a viaduct here for the Castle Douglas-Portpatrick line (The Port Road) reckoned the distance to be "only about 330 feet". It is perhaps as well that Rennie's Boat of Rhone suggestion was rejected.

More ambitious that either of those proposals was Rennie's scheme for a bridge across Loch Ken at Loup Eye. Also submitted in 1811, these plans envisaged a stone bridge of five arches crossing a waterway around 300 feet wide. In spite of its being all-stone and a longer bridge, this was priced at less than nine thousand pounds. Perhaps pricing estimates was not John Rennie's forte: nearly fifty years later the railway company's wrought iron and stone viaduct at Boat of Rhone cost them just over twelve thousand pounds, substantially less than Rennie had estimated for his structure in the same place so long before.

Sources

House of Commons	*Report of Committee on Roads between Carlisle and Portpatrick* London, 1811
Hume, J.R.	*Dumfries and Galloway; An Illustrated Architectural Guide* Edinburgh, 2000
Hume, J.R. (ed.)	*The Statistical Account of Scotland 1791-1799, Vol.V* Wakefield, 1983
Lindsay, J.	*The Canals of Scotland* Newton Abbot, 1968
Maitland, C.(ed.)	*Commissioners of Supply for the Stewartry of Kirkcudbright 1728-1828* Castle Douglas, 1933

AN INSPECTOR CALLS

A retired signals inspector with the London, Midland, and Scottish Railway Company, which operated the Galloway lines for 25 years until nationalisation in 1948, used to say that his favourite run was to Stranraer. Alighting at Dunragit, where a short stretch of double line allowed trains to pass, he would briefly inspect the signal box while the train waited and then depart, saying he would return on the next train back. When he duly did so about an hour later, the signalman always had a brace of pheasants, neatly decapitated, ready for him. At first the gratified inspector asked no questions but eventually, after many rewarding visits, he asked the signalman how the latter was able to obtain the pheasants so quickly.

The employee explained that after the inspector's first visit he would scatter Indian corn on the line so as to attract the pheasants from nearby Dunragit estate. Once the birds were feeding happily among the points, he would pull the points lever…

Source

Wallace, M.   personal communication

THE FLYING DUCHESS

The years between the World Wars are often regarded as the golden years of aviation and several women were among the pioneers of that era, one of them with a close connection with Galloway. She was Mary du Caurroy, wife of the eleventh Duke of Bedford, and was directly responsible for the family's local link. When she married her husband in India in 1888, he was an aide-de-camp to the Viceroy but, as a younger son, not heir to the dukedom. Nevertheless, as merely daughter of the archdeacon of Lahore, Mary was considered by the Bedford family to be an unsuitable bride and when the couple returned to England they were so coldly received at Woburn that they retired to Scotland, where they took a long lease of Cairnsmore estate north of Palnure between Newton Stewart and Creetown, making their first home at Cairnsmore House. Fate seemed to intend their Galloway residence to be a short one for three years later the tenant of Cairnsmore unexpectedly became Duke of Bedford on the death of his brother. With a clutch of estates in England the new duke intended to give up his Galloway lease but was persuaded to keep it on by his wife, who was a keen bird watcher and found the surrounding area gave her ample opportunities for her hobby.

The Duchess of Bedford

Initially the ducal couple travelled to Cairnsmore for their sojourns there by train, using a private railway carriage, while a posse of chauffeurs brought up the necessary Rolls Royces. And rail transport was also utilised to bring up from Woburn the Duke's personal supply of water for he would drink water from no other source (one of his manifold idiosyncracies). However, in 1926 the Duchess made a life-changing decision when she had herself flown up to Galloway, the plane landing in a field close to Cairnsmore House. The reason for the innovation was medical: the lady suffered from the ear complaint tinnitus and had been told that the changes in air pressure involved in flying brought some relief.

Although aged 60, Mary du Caurroy became an enthusiast for the youthful form of transport. She bought a plane and hired pilots to take her on attempts at the record-breaking long-distance flights so popular in those years. Her successful attempts to break the records for flights to India (return journey in seven—and-a-half days) and Australia hit the headlines and earned her the nickname of The Flying Duchess. However a passive role regarding actually piloting the aircraft no longer contented her and at the age of 62 she decided to learn to fly and obtain a pilot's licence. She continued her lessons while in Galloway on holiday, practising landings and take-offs on Luce Lands. On one occasion she landed too near the outgoing tide and the plane became bogged down in the soft sand, to be dug out by a doubtless unenthusiastic instructor.

An airfield at Cairnsmore became a necessity for the convert. The eminently suitable field near the entrance to Cairnsmore House was no longer available and so an alternative site was found over two miles away on the farm of Lennies north of Creetown. It was less than ideal as the ground was sloping and studded with rocks; 60' pylons carrying high tension electricity cables close by were undesirable neighbours. However drainage, field clearance, and the erection of a hangar and changing room seem to have made it acceptable. En route there from Woburn the Duchess used to "buzz" Cardoness and Cassencarrie Houses to wave to her friends.

Sadly Lennies airport's working life ended in 1937, when the Duchess went missing on a short flight from Woburn. No trace of her was ever found but a few pieces of wreckage from her aircraft were washed ashore near Yarmouth. However she bequeathed an aviation legacy to Galloway, not only a hangar base in a field overlooking the Cree estuary but Creetown's legitimate claim to having had the first purpose-built, fully equipped airfield for fixed-wing planes in Galloway.

A tangible relic of the building of Lennies aerodrome can be found in the Stewartry Museum at Kirkcudbright in the unlikely shape of a prehistoric axe hammer unearthed during the construction work.

Sources

Bedford, John, Duke of *A Silver-Plated Spoon* London, 1959

Connon, Peter *An Aeronautical History of the Cumbria, Dumfries and Galloway Region, Part 2* Penrith, 1984

Curtis, Lettice *Winged Odyssey* Walton-on-Thames, 1993

"KIRK AFFAIRS"

THE BIBLE, GALLOWAY VERSION

The Authorized Version of the Bible, commissioned by King James VI and I and prepared over three and a half years by 47 eminent scholars and divines, is usually regarded as an outstanding work both of scholarship and literature but this opinion was not shared by an eighteenth century native of the Glenkens, who gave practical expression to his reservations.. He was a man called Rev. James M. Ray, also known as Rev. James McCrae.

James Ray was born at Knockreoch farm in the parish of Kells in 1746, the year of the Battle of Culloden. His father subsequently moved to the farm of Woodhead north of Carsphairn, remaining there for the last 30 years of his life. Consequently young James attended Carsphairn parish school before going on to Edinburgh University and then to the ministry. Unusually, his first charge was not in Scotland but a presbyterian church across the Solway at Maryport in what is now Cumbria, a reminder of the close links across that firth in the pre-railway days.

Ill health terminated his work at Maryport and forced his return for several years to Woodhead before he took up an appointment as assistant at Buittle between Dalbeattie and Castle Douglas. In 1792 he was on the move again, this time to Edinburgh and a post as teacher of Hebrew. Here occurred the crucial event of his life when he became acquainted with a wealthy businessman, James Gillespie, who used the fortune he had made as a tobacconist to found the famous school which still bears his name. Ray became Gillespie's chaplain and companion and with him toured Europe and the United States. He was now able to communicate to the world the fruits of his academic studies. In America he gave a series of "philosophical-medical lectures" while in Scotland he lectured on a wide variety of subjects. He also published booklets on formidable topics such as *The Theories of the Origin of the Universe* and *The Philosophy of the Languages of Men, Beasts, Birds, etc.*, works dismissed by his biographer as "masses of matter capriciously huddled together".

But all this was a preliminary to the great work of his life. For Ray was profoundly dissatisfied with the Authorized Version of the Bible, considering it "the worst translated work extant and quite unintelligible in many important places". He therefore set to and produced an improved version complete with interpretative notes, *A Revised Translation and Interpretation of the Sacred Scriptures*. Although his biographer describes it as "an arbitrary paraphrase", the work seems to have proved popular for the first edition of 1799 was followed by another impression in 1815.

Ray did not return a second time to his native Glenkens. After twelve years as chaplain at Mr Gillespie's school, he moved to Glasgow, dying there in 1816. Wherever he lived he must have attracted attention by both his old-fashioned clothes and unexpectedly radical political opinions as well as commanding respect by his simple and self-denying way of life. His career has interesting parallels with that of his infinitely better known Stewartry contemporary, Alexander Murray.

Sources

Murray, T.   *The Literary History of Galloway, 2nd edn* Edinburgh, 1832

THE KEN VALLEY'S "TURBULENT PRIEST" (1)

King Henry II's famous description of Thomas Becket could surely be applied to the Rev. John McMillan, minister at Balmaghie for 28 years at the start of the eighteenth century. Born at Barncaughla farm in Minnigaff parish in 1669, he may have acquired or strengthened his strict Covenanting beliefs from the reputed fate of his neighbour, young Margaret Wilson, who tradition says was executed by drowning at Wigtown for her faith in 1685. At any rate when he went to Edinburgh University he joined a Cameronian Society, one of the groups of strict Covenanters which rejected the Revolution Settlement of 1689 because it did not make presbyterianism the established religion of the whole of Britain.

McMillan, however, quitted the "Society People" temporarily to take a theology course and become a Church of Scotland minister – and a sharp thorn in the flesh of that body. His first post as chaplain to Murray of Broughton, near Whithorn, was followed by appointment as minister of Balmaghie parish in 1701. He at once showed his colours by repeated complaints to Kirkcudbright Presbytery that the Church of Scotland had departed from strict Covenanting principles. Warned about his conduct by that body, he simply stopped attending their meetings and was consequently deposed after just two years.

The present Balmaghie church (built 1794) on the site of McMillan's building

But the Presbytery had not reckoned on the strength of McMillan's support among his parishioners. Two ministers sent formally to declare the charge vacant were prevented by McMillan adherents from entering the church. After an appeal to the civil authorities, the sheriff with 100 soldiers arrived to expel McMillan but was met by huge crowds of his followers and forced to retire. Meanwhile the offending minister continued to carry out his duties and occupy the manse as if all was normal, a state of affairs which lasted for seven years until the Presbytery appointed a new minister. An attempt supported by soldiers to induct the latter at Balmaghie church failed because of the opposition of a large and irate crowd.

The new minister, with Presbytery approval, wisely decided to avoid further confrontation by finding alternative accommodation, having a meeting-house constructed for his use near Glenlochar bridge. Matters continued thus for an extraordinary nineteen years with Balmaghie parish enjoying the services of two ministers but with McMillan in possession of the church, its manse, and its glebe. The situation was resolved only when he decided to leave the parish to preach to and serve the scattered Cameronian Societies across the southern half of Scotland. He eventually welded those into a single body, the Reformed Presbyterian Church, of which he is consequently regarded as founder.

Meanwhile in Balmaghie a relieved Presbytery saw the "minister in waiting", McKie, finally in undisputed possession of the parish, which he served for another 34 years, earning both the regard and affection of his flock.

Sources

Reid, H.   *The Kirk above Dee Water* Castle Douglas, 1895

THE KEN VALLEY'S "TURBULENT PRIEST" (2)

Over two hundred years after James McMillan created such notable turbulence in Balmaghie parish in the sphere of religion another minister, this time from the neighbouring parish of Crossmichael, created reverberations in local political affairs. As in McMillan's case his actions had national effects. The Rev. James Fisher was a complex character. A totally devout Christian with the mind of a scientist, he saw science not as the enemy of religious faith but as the ally. A combatant infantry officer in World War One and Home Guard battalion commander in World War Two, he would not permit rabbits to be shot in the glebe nor rooks in the manse wood, the latter edict a source of some local discontent.

He entered local politics in 1936 as the result of a traumatic experience suffered by his daughter in consequence of an incorrect diagnosis in a local hospital. An enraged James Fisher decided to stand for the Stewartry County Council and campaign for improved local health services. His outstanding ability as a public speaker and keen mind very soon made an impact while his determination to effect radical change in the council's policies and operating methods ensured he became a controversial figure, whose views received widespread local and national publicity. Recognition of his qualities by his fellow councillors led to his being elected Convener in 1945, a post he held until his death in 1960.

Wider recognition also came his way with the chairmanship of the Health Committee for Scotland and the presidency of the Association of County Councils in Scotland. But possibly the post that gave him greatest pleasure was the chairmanship of the county council library committee. He was a voracious reader and this position allowed him his only known piece of self-indulgence: when new books were obtained for the library he was allowed pre-issue borrowing of those that interested him. But his passion for books also ensured that the Stewartry had an excellent lending library service, as the book stock of its successor organisation still testifies.

Sources

Neville, P.   *My Father's House* London, 1969

PRECENTORS

The survival of two pulpits, an upper and a lower one, in some local churches today is a tangible reminder of the times when the precentor was a prominent figure in Church of Scotland services. The lower "pulpit" was in fact the precentor's box, his job being to start and lead the singing of the psalms and paraphrases: "lining oot" or "gien out the line" as the task was commonly described. His only musical accompaniment was a tuning fork. The precentor sang one line at a time and this was then repeated by the congregation, the earlier system of his singing the whole psalm before the congregation did likewise having been abandoned. However, some precentors apparently did not permit the congregation to sing but insisted on giving a solo performance. They also made announcements. The precentor was usually the session clerk and schoolmaster.

The reason for their existence lay in the early years of the reformed church when Bibles were scarce and even when they were available many people couldn't read. By the start of the eighteenth century the situation had changed and in 1709 it was recommended that "lining oot" should be abolished. However the advice was slow to be implemented and precentors continued to perform their duties well into the nineteenth century, when the introduction of organs finally rendered them redundant.

The post was not without its problems. It is recorded that one elderly lady announced defiantly that she "wad praise the Lord wi a her micht whether she kent the tune or no." And a tale is told that when the legendary Captain Denniston of Creetown attended service at Penninghame church with his dog, it competed with the precentor every time the latter started to sing. At the conclusion of the service the minister, elders, and precentor interviewed the captain and requested him to ensure there was no repetition. The captain agreed to do his best but helpfully commented,

"If you'll be adviset by me, ye'll pit the tyke intil the precentor's box and let it dae the precentin for if A'm ony judge o music the tyke's far an awa the better singer o the twa."

The fact that the words of the psalms and paraphrase were considered too sacred to be used anywhere but in the church service presented a problem for precentors when they took choir practice. They solved the difficulty by making up slightly different words for the tunes, which often did little to ensure respect for the originals:

"Behold! How good a thing it is,
And how becoming well,
Tae hae a great big treacle piece,

And eat it aa yersel."

"All people that on earth do dwell,
Rax oot yer hands and help yersel;
Or else, you may depend upon't,
You'll get a scone, an naething on't."

Precentors still operate today in some presbyterian denominations.

Sources

Trotter, R de B.   *Galloway Gossip; The Stewartry* Dumfries, 1901

Walker, A.A.   *Praise in Common Metre* <u>in</u> *The Quest, No. 35*
                         Dumfries, 1960

THE QUEEN, THE COLONEL, AND THE KELLS MINISTER

The embittered relations between King George IV and his estranged queen, Caroline of Brunswick, led in the early nineteenth century to a remarkable incident in the ecclesiastical history of the Stewartry after George decreed that no prayers for his wife as queen should be made in churches. In July, 1820, the Stewartry Gentlemen Yeomenry Cavalry, a militia unit, were in annual camp near Kirkcudbright. Their commanding officer, James Gordon of Culvennan, a strong king's man, invited the regimental chaplain, the Rev. William Gillespie of Kells, to take Sunday service in Kirkcudbright church, adding an enquiry as to whether the minister intended to pray for the queen. The minister's answer was equivocal but in the event he did so. An outraged Gordon promptly placed him under military arrest. This action was not as draconian as is seemed for the annual camp ended next day and with it the colonel's authority; moreover clarification of the sentence revealed that it simply meant that for the few hours involved Gillespie was not to leave the Stewartry.

However the minister chose to interpret it in the gravest light possible since he considered Gordon had interfered with the Church of Scotland's cherished freedom from interference by the civil or military power. He therefore promptly complained to the Lord Advocate, claiming that Gordon's action constituted "an invasion of the privileges, and a breach of the independence of our national church." The Lord Advocate agreed Gordon's action had been "illegal and indiscreet" and ordered him to apologise by letter. The colonel did so with a notable absence of sincerity. The whole affair attracted not merely national but international publicity: it was reported in the columns of *The Calcutta Times*.

The matter did not end with the apology for a local, anonymous author used the event as a pretext for circulating a long poem, *The Galloway Herds*, in which a number of local ministers were rather clumsily lampooned for alleged personal defects and moral irregularities irrespective of their stance on the Queen's prayer issue. Thus the Twynholm minister was pilloried for failing to turn up at an open-air service on a day of inclement weather:

"When cauld whirling drift
Drives down frae the lift,
Good shepherds aye hurry the faster;
But poor Twynholm crocks
Are a prey to the fox,
For their shepherd's a fair-weather pastor."

The poem originally existed only in a few manuscript copies until a broadsheet version was printed by a Kirkcudbright publisher. It was not until 1900 that it appeared in conventional book form. From the start the identity of the author was the subject of lively speculation with the favourite being Clauchanpluck (Laurieston) schoolmaster Samuel Sturgeon. It was also claimed that William Nicholson, the packman-poet and author of *The Brownie of Blednoch*, had a hand in it. Tradition says that Sturgeon was forced to leave the area because of his alleged authorship and emigrated to the West Indies. It was not the first nor the last time that a Galloway book has raised a storm of controversy.

Sources

Fraser, T. (ed.)　　　　　*The Galloway Herds* Dalbeattie, 1909

A HIDDEN TREASURE OF THE SOUTH RHINNS

One of the little known gems of the South Rhinns of Wigtownshire is diminutive St Agnes's chapel, tucked discreetly away down an unclassified road a mile south of Ardwell village. It was built in the late nineteenth century by James McDouall, laird of Logan, for the convenience of his estate workers and tenants since the nearest church was a considerable distance away. The chapel's only regular minister was James Gutteridge, who came to Logan House in 1872 as tutor to James McDouall's sons. A committed churchman, Gutteridge started to take episcopalian services in the chapel. Their popularity, not least with the inhabitants of Port Logan village, created a regular congregation and led to Gutteridge's being formally ordained as a clergyman. For a time after his death in 1911 regular services were maintained at St Agnes's by a rota of neighbouring ministers but a dispute with the laird led to their discontinuation. Nevertheless, occasional services on special occasions were held until not so many years ago. The chapel has been disused for some time and it is planned to convert it into a dwelling house

St Agnes's chapel

Although small, St Agnes's has crow-stepped gables and stained glass windows. Internally the walls are panelled with wood and the wooden furnishings display a high standard of craftsmanship. The woodwork is apparently the work of the estate joiner, Mr Rodie, and his sons. The fact that the chapel was built around the same time that Logan House was hugely extended (1874-78) raises the intriguing possibility that its fabric (of rubble with brick facings) was a luck-penny from the builder to the laird. This possibility is encouraged by indications that the chapel is a conversion of an agricultural building. It has no proper foundations and in the gables are traces of a blocked up door and window.

James McDouall's wife, formerly Agnes Buchan Hepburn, is prominent in the chapel's story. It was named with her in mind and the large, stained glass window in the west wall, with its *agnus dei* motif, is a memorial to her. But it is possible to speculate an even closer connection. Mrs McDouall was a member of the sect known as The Catholic Apostolic Church, frequently referred to as the Irvingites. It may not be excessively fanciful to suggest that her husband built the chapel not only for the convenience of local people but also to allow his wife to worship privately in the way she preferred. Her creed's belief that ordinary members possess the power of prophetic utterance, its open-mindedness to other faiths, and the presence in the area of fellow-adherents like Sir Herbert Maxwell of Monreith perhaps give some credence to the theory.

St Agnes even had its own adjacent manse, formed by the conversion of one of a block of two cottages a few yards from the church. The nature and disposition of the buildings on the site might thus mean that a small croft originally stood here. The whole forms a fascinating chapter in the church history of the South Rhinns.

Sources

Anonymous: *History of St Agnes Chapel* (unpublished MS)
McColm, S.A.   personal communication
Maxwell, Sir H.   *Evening Memories* London, 1932

"BLOODY INSTRUCTIONS"?

When most of us think of the politico-religious troubles that racked Scotland in the seventeenth century before the triumph of presbyterianism with The Glorious Revolution of 1688, our picture is of the royalist, episcopalian party in power and presbyterian adherents as the oppressed victims of a series of draconian laws designed to discourage their support of their chosen form of religion. While this may be true of the later part of the struggle from 1660 onwards, at an earlier stage the roles were in fact reversed. A graphic picture of this little known period emerges from the *Minute Book of the War Committee in the Stewartry of Kirkcudbright in the Years 1640 and 41*, which had been preserved in the charter chest of Sir David Maxwell of Cardoness and was published in 1855 by the Kirkcudbright printer and publisher John Nicholson.

The presbyterian ascendancy in the early 1640's resulted from reaction to Charles I's attempts to impose episcopalianism on a hostile Scotland. The National Covenant of 1638, whose multitudinous signatories pledged to defend "the true religion", was followed by the General Assembly's abolition of all the king's episcopal innovations, an action replicated soon afterwards by the Scottish parliament. Charles's attempts to reassert himself by military means were easily repelled with the victorious Scottish army moving south and occupying north-east England to encourage the monarch to come to terms.

All this required raising, equipping, and maintaining an army and this was the *raison d'etre* for local war committees such as the Stewartry version. The Southern Regiment was formed, to be manned mainly by recruits from Galloway and with a complement of 80 cavalry together with an unspecified number of infantry. Sir Thomas Maclellan, 2nd Lord Kirkcudbright, was appointed colonel; acting under him were initially four captains all drawn from different branches of the ubiquitous Gordon family. The local war committee's task was to find the necessary men, horses, and equipment and then raise the money to support them in the field. Both tasks were to prove exceedingly difficult, especially with an increasingly impatient Scottish parliament (The Estates) breathing heavily down local necks. The Estates hit upon the idea of raising part of the finance required and at the same time discouraging the holding of non-presbyterian beliefs by a series of measures against "ante-covenanters, papists and recusants".

Under those enactments, rates and other payments due to landholders in the above categories had instead to be paid to the War Committee "for the use of the public". Failure to do so meant that the offender had troops billeted on him at his expense. In addition, the crops, goods, and gear of ante-covenanters were seized and sold for the same purpose. Understandably this appears to have caused some hardship for on several occasions Margaret Brown of Bagbie near Creetown asked the committee to be allowed some of her husband's "goods and gear" for the aliment (subsistence) of her and her children. The committee, while acceding to her request, do not seem to have erred on the side of generosity and on the last occasion they informed the lady that before she received any further grant she would have to obtain a warrant from parliament. In the meantime she was reminded to continue "giving satisfaction to the kirk" (attending presbyterian service). The families of Robert Maxwell of Culnachtrie and Harry Lyndsay of Rascarrel, in the same situation, were reportedly "reduced to extreme miserie and hardness".

Margaret Brown's case also shows that freedom of worship was a casualty of the times, a fact illustrated by the experience of James Gordon of Crofts, reported for failure to sign the National Covenant, something which was by now compulsory. Freedom of speech fared no better as John Halliday of Falbae discovered when his "impertinent words" that "it was ane better world in the pretendit bischops' time than now" landed him in prison and the stocks with a fine added for good measure.

As time went on, the net widened to include additional categories of those liable to financial penalties. Early in 1841 the local war committee identified a new class of undesirable person, "The cold Covenanter", defined as "such ane persone quha does not his dewtie in everie thing committed to his charge thankfullie and willinglie, without compulsion, for the furtherance of the publict". The adverbs ensure that proving one was not in this category would be an onerous task. The definition brings to mind the line from the musical *Call Me Madam*: "When you call me Madam, smile".

While the times were certainly abnormal, it is difficult to read of those punitive measures against the non-conformists of the day without remembering the words of Macbeth in Shakespeare's great play:

" ...we but teach
Bloody instructions, which being taught return
To plague the inventor."

Sources

Nicholson, J. (ed)   *Minute Book of the War Committee in the Stewartry o
                            Kirkcudbright in the Years 1640 and 1641* Kirkcudbright,
                            1855

FRAE AA THE ARTS

JOHN NICHOLSON, LITERARY ENTREPRENEUR

William Nicholson is deservedly widely known as the author of the extraordinary *Brownie of Blednoch* but his brother John unfairly languishes in relative obscurity. His life embraced a variety of careers. Born in Tongland parish in 1778, he first became a weaver, serving his apprenticeship in New Galloway and then transferring to Glasgow. His sojourn there was punctuated by a short period of army life, when he served in the Guards. His second spell at the weaving trade was ended by an injury to his hand, which necessitated another change of direction, this time to the same calling as his brother William, that of packman in the south-west of Scotland, his stock-in-trade being books and stationery.

This phase was a form of apprenticeship to the most important role of his life for in 1820 he set himself up as printer and publisher in the town of Kirkcudbright and in that capacity made a significant contribution to Galloway studies. The work for which he is best known is *The History of Galloway* in two volumes, published in 1841. This was a collaborative venture with the Rev. William Mackenzie, English master at Kirkcudbright Academy, but sadly the nature of each man's contribution became a subject of acrimonious dispute. Eventually an introduction was added to the *History*, written by Nicholson but revised by a third party, the Tongland minister. This indicates that Nicholson provided most of the material while Mackenzie wrote the actual text. Nicholson printed and published the work and turned the material left over from it into a second book, entirely his own effort, called *Historical and Traditional Tales of the South of Scotland*. Both these titles are now regarded as essential for studies of the Galloway past.

Local historians are further indebted to Nicholson for publishing the MS minute books of two bodies who played important roles on opposite sides in the politico-religious conflicts of the seventeenth century, the episcopalian Synod of Galloway and the presbyterian War Committee of the Stewartry of Kirkcudbright. Local authors too were in his debt, including John McTaggart: Nicholson became an official stockist of the former's *Scottish Gallovidian Encyclopedia*.

At one time John Nicholson expanded his mini publishing empire into the field of newspapers by producing the *Stewartry Times* but this venture did not prosper. A local tradition says that the cause of its demise was that the publisher, unable to meet the deadline for printing the new issue, simply reprinted the previous week's offering and this was spotted by an eagle-eyed readership. It is further suggested that the deadline problem arose from too enthusiastic celebration of the successful publication of the previous week's *Times*. However, in fairness to Nicholson's memory it should be said that this suggestion is in conflict with the publisher's well known and strong religious principles. No record exists of the paper's London namesake being troubled by such difficulties – or resorting to such expedients.

The question of fairness to the memory of deceased persons dramatically arose in 1882, forty years after the publication of *The History of Galloway* and the controversy surrounding it. By this time the protagonists were long dead, William Mackenzie in 1854 and John Nicholson in 1866. However the dispute about authorship was certainly not forgotten by J. C. Mackenzie, brother of William and Kirkcudbright lawyer. Arguably a trifle belatedly, he produced a pamphlet which not only proved beyond doubt that his brother was sole author but which shredded the reputation of the departed Nicholson by demonstrating from the latter's own written notes that his educational attainments disqualified him from the author's role. Witness statements also testified to this as well as to major character defects.

While Mackenzie family honour was thus maintained, it is difficult not to feel sorry for Nicholson's son, James, a gentle, unworldly, and much liked Kirkcudbright resident, faced with the destruction of his formidable father's reputation.

Sources

Gordon, J.	personal communication
Mackenzie, J.C.	*Statement of Facts as to the Writing, Printing, and Publishing of 'The History of Galloway'* Kirkcudbright, 1882
Rain, W.	*The Late James Nicholson in The Gallovidian, Vol. II* Dumfries, 1900
Trotter, A.	*East Galloway Sketches* Castle Douglas, 1901

OSCAR KOKOSCHKA IN THE SOUTH MACHARS

House of Elrig on the South Machars moors just north of Elrig village is renowned as the childhood home of well known author Gavin Maxwell. But less well known is its association with an even more stellar figure in the world of European culture. This was the Austrian-born painter Oscar Kokoschka, one of the most important figures in twentieth century European art.

Kokoschka had left his native Austria in 1934 when an authoritarian, Nazi-friendly regime came to power and settled in Czechoslovakia, where he became friendly with Professor Emil Korner, an economist and financial director of a Krupps-owned steel works. However, after the 1938 Munich Agreement effectively gave Czechoslovakia to Germany, Kokoschka, whose work had been picked out by the Nazis for vilification, fled with his wife to London. There, in serious financial difficulty, he met up again with Korner, who had preceded him to Britain, and was rescued from near destitution by the latter's financial support. When Korner purchased House of Elrig from Sir Aymer Maxwell in 1940, he invited the Kokoschkas to stay there for extended periods so that between 1941 and 1946 the artist had six sojourns on the Elrig moors to the great benefit of his state of mind and his art.

Oscar Kokoschka and the view south towards Port William from above West Barr farm

The artistic fruits of his House of Elrig visits are several paintings and a mass of drawings done in sketchbooks with coloured pencils. The son of a neighbouring farmer remembers seeing the artist at work at his easel at the top of the heughs overlooking West Barr farm where the road from Elrig descends to join the Port William-Glenluce highway. The view from here appears in two Kokoschka paintings, *Scottish Coast* and *Loreley,* although the artist's style and purpose perhaps make identification less than obvious. The same informant and his brother remember the visitor wandering around busy with his sketchbook. On one occasion Kokoschka drew the elder of the boys while he was watering a horse at a trough in the farm steading, signed it, and gave it to the boys' mother. Unfortunately it was not treasured as hindsight would have demanded and has vanished into oblivion. Other subjects of sketches, fortunately preserved, were the landward end of Port William harbour and a ruined croft near Elrig village. Kokoschka's fondness for satirical treatment is revealed in a painting of the two tenants of nearby Corsemalzie House, whose passion for field sports met with the artist's disapproval, as *The Hunters* makes very clear.

However the satirist had a very gentle side and used to accompany the farmer's children home to Airylick from Elrig school to their great pleasure. Perhaps the simple life together with the peace and remoteness of his South Machars surroundings played an important part in restoring and nourishing Oscar Kokoschka's artistic impulses; Maxwell's famous autobiography may not be the only notable cultural creation for which lonely House of Elrig was responsible.

Sadly, as we have seen, Kokoschka's artistic output at House of Elrig did not command universal approbation among the local residents. This was again demonstrated when one of the staff at the house was about to be married. With typical generosity Kokoschka gave the couple two of his paintings, framed and signed, as a wedding present. However, the bride considered they did not fit in at all with her plans for interior decoration of the new home and they were consigned to the dustbin. Not long ago a Kokoschka painting of this period was for sale at an asking price of £80,000....

Sources

Calvocoressi, R.	*Kokoschka and Scotland* Edinburgh, 1990
Kerr, Ms. L.	personal communication
McFadzean, J.	personal communication
McFadzean, S.	personal communication

LITERARY VISITORS TO CUMSTOUN (1): THE FUGITIVE

Cumstoun House just north of Kirkcudbright on the banks of the River Tarff has played host to two notable names in the world of Scottish literature. The first occasion was at the end of the sixteenth century and the guest was Alexander Montgomerie, who has been called "the last of the great Scots Makars". His finest work is a long poem, *The Cherrie and the Slae,* written in a highly artificial medieval genre. In spite of its artifice and the complexities of its concealed meaning(s) the poem has stood the test of time because of its fine descriptions of the scenery of the river valley that forms the setting of the poem.

Cumstoun castle at the time of Montgomerie's visit

An old and persistent local tradition identifies that setting as the course of the River Dee from its junction with the Tarff for a mile upriver to the old Tongland bridge, a stretch described by C.H. Dick as " the Dee … at its grandest, a deep, dark, foam-flecked flood between precipitous, thickly-wooded banks". (Today this part of the river, locally known as "the Doachs", has been metamorphosed and tamed by the dam and attendant hydro-electric power station.) Writing in 1684 less than a hundred years after the poem's composition, Andrew Symson reported the local identification of this length of the Dee with the setting of *The Cherrie and the Slae*. The belief was repeated by the Tongland parish minister in 1792 in the *Old Statistical Account* with the additional information that Montgomerie had resided at Cumstoun Castle. And the tradition was referred to in the nineteenth century by Kirkcudbright publisher John Nicholson, presumably being the reason for his edition of the poem.

But why should a poet from an Ayrshire family, a leading member for long of the group of poets kept by King James VI at his court and a personal friend of the king, be in temporary residence on the banks of the Tarff? The answer may lie in the events of Montgomerie's turbulent life for as a convert to Roman Catholicism he became deeply involved in the machinations and schemings to strengthen the Roman Catholic cause in the decades after the Reformation in 1560. One of the most spectacular of those plots was an attempt in 1597 to seize Ailsa Craig off the Ayrshire coast for use as a stronghold and staging point for a proposed re-run of the Spanish Armada enterprise. The attempt, led by Hew Barclay of Ladyland, failed and, as a known associate of Barclay, Montgomerie was called before the Privy Council to explain himself. He failed to appear, was outlawed, and was never heard of again.

It was in that same year, 1597, that the *Cherie and the Slae* was published. So it is not impossible that the fugitive Montgomerie sought refuge in darkest Kirkcudbrightshire, provided he knew of a friendly host. And Cumstoun might have provided just such a one for at this time it was owned by the Brown family, one of whom, Gilbert Brown, was the last abbot of Dundrennan and so active in the Roman Catholic cause in south-west Scotland in the post-Reformation years that twice the General Assembly of the Church of Scotland demanded his arrest. The poem provides some textual evidence for the theory. Montgomerie's famous description:

"I saw an River rin
outouir ane craggie Rok of stane,
Syne lichtit in ane linn:
With tumbling, and rumbling,
Amang the Rochis round:

Dewalling, and falling,
Into that pit profound"

is very similar to the more prosaic 1792 *Old Statistical Account* picture of the same riverscape:

"…a train of the most beautiful cascades of broken water, tearing and roaring, over the rugged rocks with the most tremendous noise, (then) the river runs over a ridge of rock…and falls into a deep lin.".

So Montgomerie's description may indeed be of the famous, vanished "Doachs o' Tongue-Land Water", written while the poet was completing *The Cherrie and the Slae* in the temporary sanctuary of Cumstoun Castle with the sympathetic Browns.

Sources

Dick, C.H.   *Highways and Byways in Galloway and Carrick* Edinburgh, 1916

Grant, W. and Murison D. *The Scottish National Dictionary* Aberdeen, 1934

Harper, M.   *Rambles in Galloway* Dalbeattie, 1896

Hume, J. (ed.)   *The Statistical Account of Scotland 1791-1799, Vol.V* Wakefield, 1983

Lindsay, M.   *History of Scottish Literature* London, 1977

McKerlie, P.   *History of the Lands and Their Owners in Galloway, Volume Fifth* Edinburgh, 1877

McTaggart, J.   *Scottish Gallovidian Encyclopedia; A New Edition* Perthshire, 1981

Wood, H.H.   *The Cherie and the Slae* London, 1937

LITERARY VISITORS TO CUMSTOUN (2): THE NOBLE LORD

The second literary lion associated with Cumstoun did not stay in the fifteenth century tower house where Montgomerie would have lodged for it was now derelict but in the mansion house built in the early nineteenth century. He was Lord Cockburn, distinguished lawyer and judge but also famous in the literary world as the author of *Memorials of His Time*, a vivid and witty picture of Edinburgh life and society in his day, the first half of the nineteenth century. When Cockburn presided over sittings of the High Court in Ayr or Dumfries he sometimes stayed at Cumstoun with his friend Thomas Maitland, Lord Dundrennan, also a distinguished lawyer. Three visits in all gave him the opportunity to see something of Galloway and he recorded his impressions in diary form in his book *Circuit Journeys*.

Cockburn was passionately interested in the built environment and its conservation and his comments on various Stewartry towns, villages, and historical sites are well known with few likely to be quoted in Tourist Board literature. Less well known, but also the result of the application of exacting standards, are his views on some of our most cherished landscapes. Thus, the coast road from New Abbey by Colvend and Rockliffe to Dalbeattie is judged a disappointment despite its local reputation:

"(the Solway) is the stupidest of all our Firths. Few rocks, no islands, and especially no edging of picturesque mountains…the English mountains…are too far off to be felt as parts of the real picture." He is particularly severe on the tidal stretch of the Dee above and below Kirkcudbright, a popular subject with the town's well known artists: "the paltry puddle of ebbing and flowing mud, which the natives flatter themselves is the sea."

However, like Carlyle after him, he is greatly impressed by the coast road from Gatehouse to Newton Stewart with a minor reservation: the view across the estuary to Wigtown does not live up to its billing as the Machars coast is too flat. But the way from Kirkcudbright up the west side of Loch Ken to New Galloway and thence by Moniaive to Thornhill wins his unqualified approval (Moniaive village excepted) for this "half Highland country…partly agricultural and partly pastoral…better than either separately." The icing on the cake for this connoisseur of human nature was a conversation with a shepherd near Mossdale, who responded with the indignation of affronted local pride to Cockburn's enquiry if the watercourse nearby was the Tarff:

"Tarf! Deil a drap o' Tarf's in't. That's the black water o' Dee! The auncientest water in Scotland."

With the perceptive eye of the East Coast outsider the judge contrasts the "good, firm, clean, green turf" of Galloway with "the poor yellow verdure of the turf of ordinary Scotland", a characteristic of the local landscape equally true today and all too often taken for granted by the native. However, a major feature of our built environment does not win his approval:

"Granite is admirable for fortifications, bridges, or other works of eternity, where durability is the only beauty. But for houses it is too cold". Unpalatable though some of his comments may be, it is a tribute to the perspicacity of his observation that over a hundred years later he can make us look anew at our surroundings.

It is also a tribute to the perspicacity of Cockburn's observation that in spite of his strictures on the tidal stretch of the Dee close to Kirkcudbright ("dismal swamps of deep, sleechy mud") he noted the latter was "very shiny in the sun.....(with) hues enough to afford subjects for many pictures."

A hundred years later his view was endorsed by an art college graduate, a native of Whinnieliggate. She maintained that one of the main reasons so many painters had been attracted to Kirkcudbright was the visual quality of the river mud, which had a sheen created by the silicone it contained. So it might be claimed that Lord Cockburn predicted the formation of the town's famous artists' colony and a major cause of its existence long before even its first beginnings.

Sources

Cockburn, Lord H.   *Circuit Journeys,* Byway Books edn Hawick, 1983

Gifford, J.   *The Buildings of Dumfries and Galloway* London, 1996

McMurray, Mrs J.   personal communication

CAPTAIN DENNISTON, RACONTEUR EXTRAORDINARY

Captain James Denniston of Creetown, whose life spanned the late eighteenth century and first half of the nineteenth, enjoyed considerable local celebrity as a teller of tall stories, not related to deceive or impress but to entertain. He might perhaps be styled Galloway's Baron Munchausen. This gift made his company much sought after especially as several career changes had provided him with a large fund of anecdotes. His commercial experience comprised a tailoring apprenticeship in Gatehouse, the place of his birth, and a partnership in a Creetown cotton mill. Professionally he had been articled to a Kirkcudbright solicitor and was for some years town clerk of Creetown, then a recently created burgh of barony. His CV also included military service (hence his title) for as holder of a commission in the Galloway Militia he found himself virtually a full-time soldier during the frequent wars with France. His military career led to yet another new path for he enrolled at Glasgow University to obtain academic parity with some of his fellow-officers. And while his regiment was stationed in Edinburgh he became friendly with Sir Walter Scott and James Hogg.

With his particular gift it perhaps should not come as a surprise to learn that he was a keen angler (he was also a noted maker of fishing rods). His legendary talent was less obviously of value to him in his role as an antiquarian; indeed because of it his two antiquarian works *The Battle of Craignilder* and *Legends of Galloway* are better read for enjoyment than enlightenment. He did, though, make his mark in the field of history for it is claimed that the change of name of the settlement on the Cree estuary from The Ferry to Creetown was the Captain's work.

And what of his renowned ability as a raconteur? One anecdote he told, allegedly "one of the least remarkable" in his repertoire, concerned a famous horse he had. He would relate how he was mounting her after visiting Lord Selkirk at St Mary's Isle outside Kirkcudbright when he saw a rain cloud moving rapidly west towards him. He threw himself into the saddle and by galloping at full speed without pause the 25 miles to Creetown managed to stay just ahead of the rain falling heavily from it. On arriving home he threw himself from the saddle and rushed the few yards to his front door but before he could reach its shelter was thoroughly soaked!

Another tale allegedly involved his father, who had a tailor's business in Gatehouse and possessed an extensive library. From the latter he occasionally loaned books to a local lady, an enthusiastic but uncritical reader. On one occasion, wearying of her over-frequent requests for loans, Mr Denniston supposedly handed her an English dictionary, remarking she would find plenty of reading material in it. Rather to his surprise she returned it after a comparatively short time. To his enquiry as to how she had enjoyed the book, the lady replied,

"Weel, Mr Dennison, the man that wrote it kens some awfu grand words but A couldna get the threid o the story at aa."

Sources

Anonymous   *Some Galloway Glimpses* Newton Stewart, 1896
Trotter, A.   *East Galloway Sketches* Castle Douglas, 1901
Trotter, R. de B.   *Galloway Gossip, The Stewartry* Dumfries, 1901

HUGH FOSS OF BLETCHLEY PARK AND DALRY

In recent years a number of books and TV programmes have made us aware of the Second World War activities of British codebreakers at the top-secret establishment at Bletchley Park in Buckinghamshire. Their successes, particularly in cracking the supposedly unbreakable Enigma cipher, made a huge contribution to the Allied victory. One of those books, when talking about leisure activities at the centre, makes reference to a Scottish country dancing class taken by Hugh Foss. Foss had joined the Government Code and Cypher School before the outbreak of war and was by then head of the Japanese section. An informant told the book's author that Foss, a member of the Chelsea Reel Club, insisted that country dances were performed properly and that among them was *The Reel of the Fifty-First Highland Division*, famously created by two members of that body in a German P.O.W. camp.

Foss's enthusiasm for Scottish country dancing continued after the war and into his retirement. In the early 1960's he and his wife, Alison, came to live at Glendarroch just outside Dalry. By now he had turned his hobby into a small business, composing dances designed, successfully, to give pleasure to the participants and with a strong mathematical basis, which revealed his original vocation. These he published and distributed together with the music for them, some of it traditional tunes and some original work composed for the purpose. His Dalry creations are usually named after local topographical features and comprise almost a gazetteer of the Glenkens: *Earlstoun Loch, Garple Burn Reel, Kendoon Strathspey, Black Craig of Dee, Cairn Edward, The Rhinns of Kells, Airie Bennan, Polharrow Burn, Ken Bridge.*

His enthusiasm expressed itself in other ways. He wrote a history of country dancing with particular reference to the Scottish form. He also wrote authoritative and influential articles both on technique and on more general aspects of Scottish country dancing. From his pen too came humorous pieces in prose and accomplished verse including a pastiche of the *Lament for the Makaris* by the great Scottish medieval poet William Dunbar:

"The couples gather. Eightsomes form.
A shimmering calm before a storm
Stirs up to frenzy a mad sea:-
Amor saltus excitat me."

Adding to the humour of his light verse are self-deprecating comments about his maladroitness as a dancer. After his death in 1977 or 1978 many of those writings were published in a booklet called *Sundry writings anent Scottish dancing*.

Thus in a conversion of intellectual swords into ploughshares the brilliant mathematical mind that had helped unravel complex codes and ciphers in a significant contribution to winning the war turned latterly to providing pleasure for countless enthusiasts who shared his passion for a traditional Scottish leisure activity. He would surely have been pleased to know that a dance, *Glendarroch*, was created as a fitting memorial to him.

Sources

Foss, H.   *Notes on Evolution in Scottish Country Dancing* Dalry, 1973
Foss, H.   *Sundry writings anent Scottish dancing* Dalry, 1978
Hunter Mrs. S.   personal communication
Smith S.   *Station X; The Codebreakers of Bletchley Park* London, 1998

DOCTOR IN WIGTOWN

Film actor James Robertson Justice became something of a cult figure in the 1950's and 60's because of his role as idiosyncratic, irascible surgeon Sir Lancelot Spratt in the famous *Doctor* series of films, adapted from the novels of Richard Gordon. He became so closely identified with his screen persona that he was elected rector of Edinburgh University by the medical student block vote. Yet in spite of his high profile, considerable mystery surrounded the details of his life, a mystery he did little to dispel. However what is known with certainty is that for almost ten years from the early 1940's until 1950 he was a resident of the Wigtown district.

James Norval Harald Robertson Justice arrived in Wigtown during The Second World War, probably around 1943, and rented a farm cottage at Barsalloch on the Moss of Cree road between Wigtown and Newton Stewart. Initially he seems to have been on his own but was later joined by his wife, a charming and elegant lady well respected in the area. Justice himself was instantly recognizable: over six feet tall, burly, with a large beard, and usually dressed in an off-white polo neck pullover. This item of clothing led the Wigtown boys to believe he had been a submarine commander, since on war films these gentlemen were always attired thus. The assumption of a naval connection may not have been totally foolish as a former Moss of Cree farmer remembers his father being given tins of naval issue tobacco by Justice.

James Robertson Justice's cottage at Barsalloch in the 1950's.

In Wigtown he continued the assumed maritime connection, seeking to make a living from the sea by wildfowling on the Inks, and became a friend of the doyen of local wildfowlers, one-armed Robert McGuffie. He may have been the first to introduce punt gunning to the Cree estuary; he was certainly an enthusiastic practitioner. But wildfowling proved to be a precarious livelihood and it is said that on one occasion he tossed his last half-crown to determine whether to blow his brains out or struggle on. The decision was almost made for him as in the middle of winter he stripped naked to swim across a deep channel in the Inks to retrieve a shot goose that had fallen on the other side. His life was saved by the Carsenestock farmer and his wife, who staved off imminent hypothermia by immersing the shooter in mustard baths.

However his fortunes took a turn for the better (probably because of his burgeoning film career) and in 1946 he purchased the large villa "Orchardton" in Wigtown's Agnew Crescent. Here he set tongues wagging, a not unusual phenomenon, by taking out all the fireplaces in the public rooms and replacing them with a single, transportable, workman's brazier, made for him by a local blacksmith. Fuel was provided by logs about six feet long. Once the fire was kindled an end of the log was placed on it and the log simply moved up as each part was consumed. The next purchaser of "Orchardton" remembers with feeling having to install fireplaces in all the public rooms.

It was from that house that Justice issued forth during the big snow of 1947 with a pair of skis over his shoulder and proceeded to astound the locals by demonstrating his skill on the Golf Course Hill. Winter sports seemed to be a speciality of his for the son of the farmer at East Mains has clear memories of Justice skating expertly on the farm pond, using unusually long skates. But winter sports were not his only leisure activity for he soon developed an active social life among the well-to-do members of the farming community, especially those with an interest in shooting and fishing. He was also a frequent guest in the officer's mess at RAF Wigtown, better known locally as Baldoon. where his kilt, capacity for whisky, and bagpipe playing cemented his colourful reputation. No harm was done to this when he exchanged his large, ancient, green car for an even larger but equally venerable Rolls Royce. This he drove around in such an aristocratic style that a local lady recollects how as a small girl she felt she ought to curtsy when he passed. But the Rolls Royce owner was strongly and very openly left-wing in politics and was fond of saying that he would convert the vehicle into an armoured car when the Revolution came.

In 1950 Justice sold his Wigtown home and moved south presumably to be closer to the film studios for he was now established as an actor. Unfortunately in the excitement of the move he omitted to wind up all his local financial affairs, much to the regret of at least one Wigtown tradesman. He did return fleetingly once or twice, calling on one occasion at "Orchardton" but declining to enter the house. Thereafter Wigtonians had contact with their former neighbour only vicariously by visiting the local Rex cinema. There they noted with some surprise that Justice on the screen looked and behaved exactly the same as Justice in real life. However the impact of this exotic bird of passage had been so profound that even today over fifty years later his name will evoke instant recognition and a host of memories from the town's older residents.

Sources

Cameron, J.   personal communication
Lawson, B.   personal communication
McKie, Mrs. M.   personal communication
McKie, R.   personal communication
Maltman, Ms. M.   *Orchardton* in *Wigtown's Historic Buildings* Wigtown, 2004
Scoular, J.   personal communication

WANDERING WILLIE'S TALE: MADE IN GALLOWAY

Wandering Willie's Tale, embedded in Scott's novel *Redgauntlet*, is hailed by *The Oxford Companion to English Literature* as "a perfect example of the short story". It should therefore be a considerable satisfaction to local pride that a substantial part of this miniature gem is based on Galloway material. This was supplied to Scott by Joseph Train, the dedicated antiquary, whose day job as an excise officer saw him stationed at different times at Castle Douglas, Newton Stewart, and Wigtown.

The plot of the *Tale* (which might be described as *Doctor Faustus* with a happy ending) is founded on the alleged experiences of a New Abbey farmer, tenant of Grierson (or Grier) of Lag, while one of the two main characters, Sir Robert Redgauntlet, a "red-hot prelatist with commissions of lieutenancy…to put down a' the Whigs and Covenanters in the country" is based on the notorious seventeenth century persecutor himself. The historical prototype of Wandering Willie, blind itinerant fiddler, narrator of the *Tale*, and minor but memorable character in the novel, was a blind Welsh harper and fiddler, William ap Prichard, who with his family for many years lived a nomadic existence in south-west Scotland providing entertainment on rural social occasions for the ordinary folk of the area.

Unlike Scott's *Tale* the ap Prichard story does not have a happy ending. In April, 1816, the entire family of two parents and five children perished when, unable to obtain accommodation, they took shelter in a gravel pit on the outskirts of Twynholm. During the night part of the lip of the pit collapsed on the sleeping family, suffocating them all. The only survivor of the tragedy was the family donkey used to pull a small cart and left a little distance from the pit. It was the animal's braying which alerted locals to the unhappy event.

Train was in a particularly good position to furnish details of the deceased musician to Scott as he had encountered the family near Machermore outside Newton Stewart only two days before their deaths, where the harper's playing had attracted a crowd of local people and led to an impromptu dance. After the publication of *Redgauntlet* Scott orally acknowledged to Train the origins of Wandering Willie and stated his intention of erecting a memorial to the ap Prichard family in Twynholm churchyard, where they had been buried in an unmarked grave at the expense of the kirk session. However he did not do so nor did he acknowledge the connection in the introduction to any of the editions of the novel.

The omission was partly rectified in 1871, when the ministers of the four adjoining parishes erected a headstone over the family's grave at their own expense.

Acknowledgement of the *Redgauntlet* connection had to wait until 1946 when the Galloway Association of Glasgow erected a small stone on the grave recording the link with Scott's novel. In the interim, memory of the tragedy at least was kept alive in the area by a belief that the location, almost opposite the old mill at Twynholm, was haunted and by it being grimly known by the name of the Harper's Hole.

Sources

Glasgow Herald	issue of March 14th, 1946
Harvey, Sir P. (comp.)	*The Oxford Companion to English Literature, 3rd edn* Oxford, 1958
Patterson, J.	*Memoir of Joseph Train* Glasgow, 1857
Scotsman	issue of 25th April, 1946

MUSICIAN ON THE MOORS

One of the best known figures in twentieth century British music was the celebrated conductor Sir Adrian Boult. He became musical director of the BBC in 1930 and first conductor of its Symphony Orchestra. In those positions and with an international reputation he exercised a major influence in shaping the musical policy of the BBC. The great man had a modest and reluctant connection with Galloway through his father, Cedric Boult.

Boult senior, a wealthy businessman with property in Cheshire and Hampshire, was drawn to this area by his enthusiasm for field sports. Initially he leased Glencaird estate near Bargrennan from the Earl of Galloway but in 1910 he purchased the moorland Lagafater estate, consisting of four small sheep farms and Lagafater Lodge, in the upper valley of the Main Water of Luce fifteen miles north of Glenluce. Cedric Boult came to his sporting estate only in August and September for the grouse shooting, bringing with him a small army of servants from one of his English houses. They were transported by a special carriage on scheduled services to be deposited, probably in a disorientated state, at lonely Glenwhilly station. To facilitate the last stage of their journey and avoid the circuitous route by way of New Luce, their employer built a road across the trackless moor from the station to Lagafater. The wondering locals christened it The New Road.

Sir Adrian Boult visited Lagafater when his father was in residence but apparently with considerable reluctance and consequently for the minimum time required to maintain a harmonious relationship. Cedric Boult, however, always marked his son's presence by inviting neighbours to a shoot on the moors. Adrian dutifully participated but found an unusual way to show his lack of enthusiasm. While the shooting party were waiting for the beaters to direct a flight of grouse towards them, the conductor passed the time by using his gun as a baton to conduct an imaginary orchestra, much to the alarm of his fellow sportsmen. It is doubtful if the virtuoso ever displayed his skill to a less appreciative audience.

However, Sir Adrian embraced the rural life in one way, which none of the local residents would have dreamt of emulating. A burn runs just beside Lagafater Lodge and he instructed the estate gamekeeper to enlarge a small pool in it and then took a Spartan morning bathe there. His bathing place is still known as Adrian's Pool. Not far away is a small spring called Landers's Well. Landers was an Irish drainer who came every summer to Lagafater to practise his trade on the estate moors, living in a small hut beside the spring. The existence in close proximity of those two place names commemorating respectively a world-famous conductor and a seasonal, migrant worker is surely testimony to the democratic instincts of Gallovidians.

Sources

Campbell, R.   personal communication

McDowall, J.   personal communication

Lonely Lagafater Lodge.

IN THE WARS

CORUNNA AND CORSEWALL

It seems at first strange that a major 19th century military hero with no link with Galloway except a posthumous one should be commemorated by a prominent landscape feature on the shores of Loch Ryan in the west of the region.

The hero is Sir John Moore and his Galloway connection is certainly not at first sight obvious for neither he nor his family came from the area. He was, in fact, born in Glasgow, the son of a doctor, and became a career soldier at the age of 15, serving in the American War of Independence. When war broke out with revolutionary France in 1793, Moore saw active service in five different theatres, being frequently wounded. While his readiness to be in the thick of the fight made him very popular with his men, he also gained a reputation as perhaps the best trainer of infantrymen the British army has ever seen. It is a measure of his stature that many considered him the equal or even the superior of his contemporary, the great Duke of Wellington. Yet today the latter is a household name and Moore almost forgotten.

The stage was set for Moore's most celebrated achievement in 1808 during the Peninsular War when he was sent with 10,000 men to reinforce the British army in Portugal, being soon afterwards promoted to commander-in-chief. Interestingly, the man he replaced, Sir Hew Dalrymple, had a Galloway connection as the great-grandson of the first Lord Stair and later Baronet of High Mark outside Stranraer. However the supreme command proved a poisoned chalice when Moore was ordered to advance from Lisbon to assist the Spanish army defending Madrid. On approaching that city, he learned that it had fallen, the Spanish army had disintegrated, and Napoleon had cut off his line of retreat to Portugal. Thus Moore found himself in a situation very similar to that of the British Expeditionary Force in France in 1940.

To save his endangered army, Moore decided to retreat to the port of Corunna on the extreme north-west tip of Spain, where his transport ships could collect him. This entailed a journey of 250 miles over mountainous country in midwinter in appalling weather of rain and snow, harassed all the way by the pursuing French. In one of the great fighting retreats of military history, lasting three weeks, Moore led his exhausted army to Corunna only to find that to win time for his men to embark he had to drive back the pursuing French army under the formidable Marshal Soult. This he did in a desperate battle on January 16th, 1809, which cost the French 2000 men. However, Moore, as always in the thick of the fight, was mortally wounded by cannon shot and died soon after victory had been achieved. Before the British army embarked he was hastily and secretly buried as described in the celebrated poem by the Irish author Charles Wolfe:

"We buried him darkly at dead of night,
The sods with our bayonets turning,
By the struggling moonbeam's misty light
And the lantern dimly burning."

Today he lies in a granite tomb overlooking Corunna harbour. He is also commemorated nearer home for he was the first man to have a statue erected in his honour in George Square in his native city of Glasgow. It stands on the west side of that square close to the former main post office.

But what about his Galloway connection, albeit posthumous? It has to be conceded that the link is indirect. Around 1810 the Corsewall estate in the north Rhinns was sold by the Earl of Galloway in two parts. The smaller, East Corsewall estate, was purchased by a Glasgow banker Robert Carrick, who earned some degree of literary immortality by receiving mention in John Galt's great novel *The Entail*. Carrick was effective owner of The Ship Bank of Glasgow and a great admirer of the hero of Corunna. As a mark of his esteem, when he died in 1821 he left East Corsewall to the general's younger brother, James, the only condition being that the latter should add the surname Carrick to his own and become James Carrick Moore. James was succeeded in Corsewall by his son John, a great friend of that giant of Galloway culture Sir Herbert Maxwell. In fact, part of the Maxwell honeymoon was spent at Corsewall. As John Carrick Moore left no children, on his death the estate passed into other hands as dictated by Carrick's will.

It was therefore either James or John Carrick Moore who was responsible for one of the best known features of the landscape round Loch Ryan, the Ace of Clubs Wood on the grassy slopes of the Clachan Heughs overlooking the loch just north of Kirkcolm. Although visible from many places round the loch, it is best viewed from the Irish ferry or the picnic area at the north end of Cairnryan. Its name perfectly describes its shape and local tradition claims that shape represents the formation adopted by the British army at the Battle of Corunna, the wood being the Carrick Moores' way of commemorating their distinguished relative's greatest achievement. Unfortunately for local lore, the British army at Corunna adopted a conventional formation with four brigades drawn up in a straight line across the field of battle. Yet the tradition is almost correct: Moore lined up his army on the southern slopes of an irregular ridge or area of high ground, which in shape roughly resembles an ace of clubs, its highest part being the summit called Monte Mero. The southern slopes form the base of the ace. This information would be readily available from any of the numerous books about the Peninsular War.

And so perhaps a statue in the centre of Glasgow and an eye-catching wood dominating a south-western sea loch go some little way to meeting Moore's dying wish:

"I hope my country will do me justice."

Sources

McKerlie, P.   *History of the Lands and Their Owners in Galloway, Volume First* Edinburgh, 1870

Maxwell, Sir H.   *Evening Memories* London, 1932

Napier, W.   *History of the War in the Peninsula, Vol. 1; 3rd edn* London, 1992

FROM THE GLENKENS TO FLANDERS FIELDS

Emigration from Galloway to Australia, Canada, and New Zealand, particularly by members of the farming community, is a tradition going back over 150 years. So it was not an uncommon event when in 1849 the McCrae family of Carsphairn decided to seek a better future on the other side of the Atlantic in Canada. With David McCrae, aged 49, and his wife Marion went their five children and several grandchildren. One of the latter, aged four, was also called David and had been born in the village of Laurieston near Castle Douglas.

The McCrae extended family settled in the town of Guelph in Ontario, where David Senior went into lumbering and then moved into the woollen industry, setting up a highly successful mill. Eventually he bought some Galloway cattle and founded a herd, which soon became nationally renowned. Laurieston-born grandson David in his turn also became a noted breeder of Galloway cattle. In addition he was a highly successful businessman, who became head of The North American Life Insurance Co. But his great passion lay elsewhere, in soldiering with the local militia.

This latter enthusiasm was inherited by his second son, John, although like his father John did not become a professional soldier. Instead he pursued his martial inclinations again through the militia while obtaining two university degrees, firstly in arts and afterwards in medicine. It was in the latter field that he made his career as a GP then as a surgeon and later as a university lecturer. However, he maintained his contact with the arts by writing occasional poetry.

John McCrae's military enthusiasm led him to volunteer for service in The Boer War and again in 1914 when The Great War broke out. He was sent to France with the Canadian Medical Corps in 1915 and was in charge of a front-line dressing station during the Second Battle of Ypres in the spring of that year, when poison gas was used by the Germans for the first time. His dressing station was a dugout in the embankment of the Ypres canal near Essex farm so close to the front line that when men were shot they literally rolled down the embankment into McCrae's post.

It is extraordinary to think of writing poetry in such conditions but in the brief intervals between the arrivals of batches of wounded McCrae wrote a short poem on paper torn from a dispatch book. The subject was not the escapist one of his father's native Galloway but the current reality of Flanders. Friends to whom he showed it were impressed and asked for copies, which circulated and were much sought after. As a result McCrae was persuaded to send his poem to the magazine *Punch*, whose literary editor was so taken with it that he not only published it but did so in the heavy, black type which the magazine reserved for contributions of special note. The poem begins:

"In Flanders fields the poppies blow
Between the crosses, row on row,
That mark our place; and in the sky
The larks, still bravely singing, fly
Scarce heard amid the guns below."

John McCrae had written what was to become, and remains, the most famous poem of The First World War, familiar to millions not only in Britain and Canada but also on the Continent. In Bruges, bookshops stock a biography of McCrae, *In Flanders Fields*, in English, French, and Flemish versions, while a recorded reading of the poem is a central feature of the In Flanders Fields Museum in the famous reconstructed Cloth Hall at Ypres. And it was McCrae's poem that inspired the idea of the poppy as the symbol of remembrance.

John McCrae

The author did not live to see all this and is not buried in Flanders fields. He died in military hospital in Boulgone in January, 1918, of a lung infection with complications, a legacy of the 1915 Ypres gas attacks. But it is surely a matter for local pride that the symbolical red flower worn on Remembrance Day by tens of thousands is the result of a short poem written by the son of a native of Laurieston in Galloway.

Sources

Clendenan, M.   *The McCraes of Carsphairn* <u>in</u> *The Gallovidian, 1938*
                       Dumfries, 1938

Verleyen, H.   *In Flanders Fields* Veurne, Belgium, 1995

A FAMILY AT WAR

When The First World War broke out in August, 1914, the War Office immediately launched a campaign to recruit one million volunteers (conscription was still some way off) to augment Britain's small, professional army, "the army of mercenaries" as the Kaiser called them with grossly misplaced contempt. . The call was handsomely answered by the McGuffie family of 1 North Main Street, Wigtown, whose four sons all enlisted in the early days of the war. Thomas, the eldest, and Robert, the youngest, both joined The Royal Scots Fusiliers, while the second son, John Edward, chose The Cameron Highlanders. However, the third son, Louis, was already a member of 'H' Company of the 5th Battalion (TA) of The King's Own Scottish Borderers with its HQ at Newton Stewart's Victoria Hall and so it was in that battalion and regiment that Louis went to war.

The conflict was to demand a heavy price from the McGuffie family. In December, 1915, Private Louis was wounded while serving with the Mediterranean Expeditionary Force at Gallipoli in the Dardanelles. Perhaps the stress of having four sons on active service had something to do with the sudden death in October, 1917, of Edward McGuffie, a labourer and well known figure in the county town: he was in his early 60's. And the price continued to be paid. Less than a year later, in September, 1918, youngest brother Robert, previously wounded on several occasions, was severely wounded and lost his left arm on the Somme. About the same time John Edward was invalided out of the forces. And that autumn brought further sacrifice.

Louis McGuffie V.C.

For the 1st/5th KOSB had been ordered to Flanders and to one of the most dangerous places on earth, the notorious Ypres salient, to take part in the great Allied offensive of autumn, 1918. And so Corporal Louis McGuffie found himself in the south of that salient in an area where several names that were to become household ones in World War Two were also serving: Colonel Winston Churchill; a young American officer called George Patten;

and a German corporal by the name of Adolf Hitler. It was here that, in the words of the regimental historian, Louis McGuffie "immortalised himself and his regiment by his valour."

In the early morning of 28th September, while elements of the 1st/5th Battalion were attacking Piccadilly Farm, McGuffie's platoon commander was killed. McGuffie took command and single handed captured several enemy dugouts, forcing 28 Germans to surrender. Shortly afterwards, while the company was regrouping, he saw a party of 40 British prisoners being led off by a German escort. He dashed out, disarmed the escort, again single handed, and released the prisoners. Later in the day, when machine gun fire from a pillbox was holding up the advance, the corporal ran forward and fired several rifle grenades through the loopholes, thus enabling the strongpoint and its occupants to be captured. But six days later, on 4th October, before these exploits of stunning bravery could be officially recognized, Acting Sergeant McGuffie was killed by shellfire, five weeks before the Armistice.

It is to be hoped that Mrs McGuffie's grief at the loss of her son was slightly assuaged in mid-December when it was announced that Louis had been awarded the highest honour that a British serviceman or servicewoman can achieve, the Victoria Cross, for "most conspicuous bravery and resourceful leadership under heavy fire". In May, 1919, she travelled to London and on Saturday, the 17th, received her son's medal from the king at an investiture at Buckingham Palace.

Her return to Wigtown on the Monday evening was a memorable one. Wearing her son's medal, she was met at the station by Provost Shaw and other dignitaries. She and the provost were then conveyed by pony and trap in a procession led by the town band through crowd-lined streets to her home in North Main Street. While she went indoors to receive the Earl of Stair, Provost Dyer of Stranraer, and other notables, the large crowd outside was entertained by the town band and then thrilled when a neighbour, Mrs Savage, brought out the famous bronze medal in its presentation box and walked through the throng to let people see it.

But away from the band, crowds, and visiting dignitaries Mrs McGuffie had to contend not only with her emotional loss but also at a material level with the loss from her family of two breadwinners and the handicapping of two others (although one-armed Robert, "Duckins", was to become a wildfowler of legendary skill on Wigtown's Inks). Some idea of what that entailed can be glimpsed from a report of the unveiling in December, 1920, of a memorial tablet to Louis McGuffie in Wigtown County Buildings. On that occasion thanks were given to subscribers to the Mrs McGuffie Fund. One hopes they were numerous and generous and that the fund gave

Mrs McGuffie some financial security; she had paid a heavy price for her family's ready response to Kitchener's 1914 call "Your Country Needs You". She might well have echoed, with appropriate amendment, the words of another bereaved parent, Rudyard Kipling:

"If blood be the price of admiralty
Lord God we ha' paid in full."

Sources

Gardiner, G.	personal communication
Gillon, S.	*The KOSB in the Great War* London, 1930
Scott-Elliott, W.	*The War History of the 5th Battalion KOSB* Dumfries, 1928
Wallace, W.	personal communication
Wigtownshire Free Press	various issues 1915-1920

HOME IS THE SOLDIER?

A glance at any war memorial will make clear the heavy toll exacted by The First World War on every parish in the land. Consequently news of the death of a local person on active service was no novelty. Nevertheless particular sadness was felt in Wigtown in November, 1916, when news spread of the death on the 24th of that month of Ernest McClelland of Glenturk, one of four brothers serving in the armed forces. Ernest, a Cameron Highlander, had died in a casualty clearing station on the Western Front of wounds received in action five days previously. His loss was felt with particular keenness as he had returned to the front only a few weeks before after being severely wounded the previous September.

When the news arrived in Wigtown that late November day, it was the main topic of conversation on the streets of the burgh. As one group stood discussing the unwelcome event, an old gangin bodie, a tramp woman, stopped to listen and caught the dead man's name.

"Ernest McClelland!" she exclaimed. "A saa him last nicht on the road."

"Don't be silly, Maggie," said one of the group. "You weren't listening to what we were saying. Ernest McClelland died in France several days ago."

"Maybe so," said the old tramp, "but A saa him last nicht jist at the darknin. When A was comin up the Wigtown Hill, he was comin doon, headit for Glenturk. An his face shone like a star…"

Source

Vance, Mrs. C.   personal communication

THE LOCH DOON SCANDAL

Galloway has played host to a number of Armed Forces firing ranges but none more remarkable than the one planned in The First World War for Loch Doon on the Ayrshire-Galloway border. In 1916 the War Department decided to establish there an aerial gunnery school for Royal Flying Corps and Royal Naval Air Service personnel. Targets mounted on electrically powered bogies would descend the steep slopes on the east (Galloway) side of the loch by a zig-zag monorail, replicating the manoeuvring of enemy aircraft in a dog fight, and thus allow the fledgling pilots to hone their gunnery skills. Local objections on the grounds of weather and terrain were ignored and a massive construction project began, which at its peak involved 3,000 men, including hundreds of German P.O.W's.

A large hangar was built at the lochside to accommodate RNAS seaplanes and work began to convert an unpromisingly boggy stretch of level ground on the west side of the loch into an airfield. Six months and many thousands of pounds later the airfield project was abandoned and instead a replacement constructed between Dalmellington and Bogton Loch to the west of that town. It boasted two centrally heated hangars and barracks for 500 men but was dwarfed by the accommodation at Loch Doon, intended for a population of 1,500 and listing among its facilities a 400-seat cinema. In case all this did not fully occupy main contractors R. McAlpine and Sons, a light railway from Dalmellington part of the way to Loch Doon was commissioned and, as icing on the cake, a dam was constructed across the latter loch to raise its level by six feet to provide the necessary water for a hydro-electric power station.

Belatedly alarm bells began to ring in government circles at the huge expenditure all this involved and a Select Committee was set up to investigate. It bleakly noted the unsuitability of a site where flying would be possibly for only half the year and the fact that the frequent freezing of the loch in winter was unhelpful to the operation of seaplanes. The 60mph maximum speed of the target-carrying bogies was not felt to reflect actual dogfighting conditions in 1917. The Committee concluded that the enterprise "was misconceived from the beginning and…ought never to have been continued." Thereafter the curtain was hastily brought down in early 1918 on the ill-starred project, which never became operational, and today few physical traces remain of the works, which probably cost more than £3 million in the monetary values of that time. Perhaps it smacks of cynicism to see the Loch Doon aerial gunnery school as a dummy run for the Holyrood parliament building 80 years later.

Sources

Connon, Peter — *An Aeronautical History of the Cumbria, Dumfries and Galloway Region, Part 2* Penrith, 1984

Strawhorn, John <u>and</u> Andrew, Ken — *Discovering Ayrshire* Edinburgh, 1988

BEE PILOTS

During The Second World War a Heavy Anti-Aircraft Practice Camp was situated at Burrowhead just north of the Isle of Whithorn. As well as firing at targets towed by aircraft, for the first three years of the war the tyro gunners were also able to practise by shooting at pilotless, radio-controlled Tiger Moth biplanes known as Queen Bees. Initially these were fitted with floats and launched from a ship's catapult at Burrowhead, landing in the sea off Isle of Whithorn at the end of the mission. Later a flight of two was operated from a grass airstrip at Kidsdale two miles north of Isle of Whithorn by a unit which included on its strength two pilots.

Queen Bee on the range

The job of the latter was to take the aircraft on regular, manually-controlled, test flights and check the radio-control equipment to ensure it was working properly. Needless to say, on those occasions no shooting took place. However, the whole operation of Queen Bees was little understood by the local population. All they knew was that, while a Queen Bee was rarely directly hit, shells frequently burst very close to the aircraft, which consequently suffered considerable damage. (In fact, between August, 1939, and April, 1942, 32 of the biplanes were lost.)

One evening soon after the first Queen Bees had arrived at Kidsdale, the two pilots decided to walk into Isle of Whithorn to sample the hospitality of the famous Steam Packet Hotel on the quay. On settling themselves in the bar, they were engaged in conversation by some local residents, who noticed the wings on their tunics.

"Ye're pilots then? Whereaboots are ye stationed?"

"Up at Kidsdale. We've just arrived."

"At Kidsdale! Dae ye fly thae planes that the Burrowheid gunners try tae shoot doon?"

"Well, yes, we do."

The two pilots did not have to buy a drink all evening.

Sources

Braby, A.	personal communication
Murchie, T.	*The RAF in Galloway, 1st edn* Wigtown, 1992
Scoular, J.	personal communication

WHEN ALL ROADS LED TO GLENLOCHAR

The traveller passing through the modest clachan of Glenlochar on the B795 at the south end of Loch Ken would probably be reluctant to believe that on the east side of the river is the site of the largest settlement that has ever existed in the Stewartry but this indeed is the case. Even more improbably we have to go back almost two thousand years to reach the period of Glenlochar's great days. During the Roman occupations of south-west Scotland in the first and second centuries a succession of four forts more or less on the same site stood on the east bank of the Dee at this point. The permanent garrison, consisting of both infantry and cavalry, amounted to around a thousand and to this must be added the civilian population of the settlement that straggled along the roads leading to the fort. This would include soldiers' dependants and those who provided goods and services of various kinds for the garrison. An annexe to the fort on the north side was probably used to house an industrial site and a bath house.

But all this would produce a population of just over one thousand, similar to modern Gatehouse and dwarfed by today's Dalbeattie, a community of around 4,500. What boosted the Glenlochar population was a series of temporary camps, at least five in number, on overlapping sites close to the fort. These were occupied, each probably for one night only, by Roman forces on the march making use of the security offered by the permanent installation. The largest, 31 acres in extent, must have been used for a legion consisting of 5,000 men and a similar number of auxiliaries. On this occasion the combination of permanent and temporary residents gave Glenlochar a population of over 11,000 and allows it to claim the accolade accorded in the opening sentence.

But why should such a huge military complex have existed here? The answer lies in the site's geographical position. At this point the key Roman road west from Dumfriesshire bifurcated, with one branch going up the Ken-Dee valley to Ayrshire and the other crossing the Dee to head west by way of Gatehouse and its fortlet, the Corse of Slakes, then Glenluce with its temporary camp, to the shores of Loch Ryan and a port probably at Innermessan. Glenlochar was therefore an important communications centre on routes much used by Roman forces. It also defended the bridge across the Dee.

However one major objection to the clachan's claim to fame suggests itself. The record-achieving population was reached for a very short time, probably for one night only. This surely invalidates the claim or paves the way for a counter-bid from the Wickerman Festival. But features of a Roman temporary camp make a legitimate case for its settlement status, however brief. It was no casual or haphazard affair but laid out to a standard, detailed plan followed almost to the letter all over the Roman empire. Every tent literally had its allotted place. Internally the camp had an elaborate layout of streets each with its name, as had each section. As for its external features, they must have seemed alarmingly permanent to the astonished indigenous residents. The camp, usually rectangular in shape, was protected by a V-shaped ditch with inside it a rampart of the earth from the excavation faced with turf. To complete the defences the bank was topped with a palisade of stakes, two of those forming the kit of each soldier. High standards of ditch digging and rampart building were maintained with care being taken to achieve the recommended profile for each. Acceptable depths and heights were laid down in military manuals: the ditch could be a formidable sixteen feet wide and ten deep The four entrances to the camp sensibly received special attention. In the absence of gates a complex arrangement of ditches and banks ensured access problems for uninvited guests. It is not surprising that a Roman military writer commented of troops on the march,

"They seem to carry a fortified city with them wherever they go."

Even if mobile, a fortified city surely qualifies as a settlement.

Sadly but unsurprisingly Glenlochar's credentials are not enhanced by a site visit. Of the plethora of temporary camps nothing is visible on the ground; cropmarks on aerial photographs are the only, if undeniable, proof of their existence. Matters are only a little better with the fort. One or two stretches of low mound and shallow ditch between the last houses on the south side of the road and the bridge are all that remain of its massive structures. As a consolation prize a few objects from the site can be found in local museums. Numerous fragments of pottery perhaps do less to fire the imagination than a set of lead weights and a fine piece of decorated horse harness.

In Rudyard Kipling's poem *The Roman Centurion's Song* a veteran of many years service in Britain is devastated to learn that his cohort has been recalled to Rome and begs his superior officer to allow him to stay:

"For me this land, that sea, these airs, those folk and fields suffice.
What purple Southern pomp can match our changeful Northern skies,
Black with December snows unshed or pearled with August haze –
The clanging arch of steel-grey March, or June's long-lighted days?
....
Here is my heart, my soul, my mind – the only life I know.
I cannot leave it all behind. Command me not to go!"

It is irresponsibly fanciful but pleasant to speculate that perhaps these sentiments were shared by some long-serving Glenlochar NCO who had put down deep roots in the uncompromising landscape of Galloway.

Sources

Hunter, F.   personal communication

Keppie, L.   *Scotland's Roman Remains*   Edinburgh, 1986

Maxwell, G.   *The Romans in Scotland*   Edinburgh, 1989

Richmond, I. <u>and</u>
St Joseph, J.   *The Roman Fort at Glenlochar* in TDGNHAS
                              Third Series,Vol. XXX   Dumfries, 1953

One of the gateways at Glenlochar fort (reconstruction).

FOLK LORE

BEWARE THE HARE

Galloway, especially its more secluded areas, is rich in folk lore. Beliefs in witchcraft are not, of course, a local prerogative nor is the particular conviction that witches frequently assumed animal form. However, what does seem characteristic of this area is the idea that the metamorphosis was into the form of a hare. Alleged instances of this phenomenon are found all over the region. In Kirkmaiden parish in the South Rhinns of Wigtownshire a young man, long absent from home, returned for New Year and on that day went shooting on Inshanks moor. Sighting a hare, he fired several times at it, each time hitting it but to no apparent effect. He then decided this must be one of the notorious Kirkmaiden witches and searched his pockets for a silver coin he could use as ammunition since silver shot is the only effective type against witches. While he was doing so, he was surprised to be addressed by the hare, which asked him if he was intending to shoot his own mother. Understandably astonished, the young man desisted, returned home, and retired to bed, where he remained until the death of his mother five years later.

Two farmworkers near Kirkcudbright also had a disconcerting encounter with an ambiguous hare. They were taking two carts of hay into that town and near the clachan of Whinnieliggate had to pass a house on the roadside occupied by an old lady with the reputation of being a witch. The two youths didn't give "the crack o a coo's thumb" for witches and so when old Jean appeared at the door to question them closely about their errand they were less than polite. However, shortly afterwards as they were going down a wooded glen, a hare ran across the road right under the horses' noses and proceeded to repeat the manoeuvre until the animals took fright and backed away so that they and the loaded carts went over the edge of the highway and down the bank. Two chastened young men had to walk into Kirkcudbright to seek assistance.

A resident of Dundrennan recounted to a late nineteenth collector an incident from his own experience when a hare ran along the street of that village, which was soon after afflicted by an epidemic of an unspecified disease. More usual was the experience of a herd named McQueen from near Corsock, who, like so many others, encountered a hare invulnerable to the shots he fired at it until, wearied of the harassment, the animal introduced a novel ending to the pattern by simply disappearing into thin air.

Another close encounter with a hare, this time in the Glenkens (where the Witch o Hannayston favoured the white hare option), involved two notable protagonists, Lord Kenmure and the notorious Witch o Drooth, a tiny clachan on the New Galloway-Moniaive road beyond the Lochinvar roadend, perhaps on the site of the modern settlement of Corriedoo. On a shooting expedition his lordship's dogs set up a white hare, an old adversary, which Kenmure had unsuccessfully bombarded on numerous occasions. This time, however, the laird had his tactics worked out and put among the lead shot a silver button which he cut off his waistcoat. The move worked: the hare yelped and ran limping towards the clachan of Drooth with hunter and dogs in close pursuit. Arriving at its destination, the hare leapt through a conveniently open window in the witch's house, leaving a trail of blood on the whitewashed windowsill. Kenmure smashed down the locked door to find the lady sitting with a blood-covered button in one hand while with the other she used a darning needle to remove lead shot from her leg.

The understandably exultant laird pointed out to the witch that she had been caught literally red-handed and would suffer the statutory fate of being burned in a tar-barrel. However, the resourceful lady reminded Kenmure that he was indebted to her for favours done in a time of difficulty and so a compromise was reached. The matter would not be reported and The Witch o Drooth would restrict her activities to other estates. Nonetheless, it would be inadvisable for travellers on the New Galloway-Moniaive road to run over a hare, especially a white one.

Sources

Gregor, Dr W.   *Folklore in Galloway* in *Annual Report of the British Association, 1897* London, 1897

Trotter, R.   *Lowran Castle* Dumfries, 1822
Trotter, R. de B.   *Galloway Gossip, The Stewartry* Dumfries, 1901
Wood, J. M.   *Witchcraft and Superstitious Record in the South-Western District of Scotland* Dumfries, 1911

MOTTES AND MONSTERS

An old, traditional tale which hovers on the outer limits of credibility occurs in two locations in the Stewartry in slightly different form. According to it, a huge serpentine animal, dragon, snake, or worm, occupied the dry ditch of a large motte, the earthen base on which a medieval wooden castle was built. The phenomenon was, in the eloquent words of a Glenkens author, "white as the snow on the hill, fierce as the wild boar in the wood, and tall as the tufted fir on the mountain's brow". At Dalry, the White Snake occupied the entire length of the ditch round the motte beside the Ken while at the larger Motte of Urr north of Dalbeattie the dragon had to wind itself seven times round the hillock in order to be accommodated. The creature's carnivorous diet made it an unwelcome neighbour but those attempting to evict it were "joost cransh't up like as mony carrots". The beast eventually became so untidy in its eating habits that anything (or anyone) smaller than a bullock was simply swallowed whole.

This was to be the animal's undoing for a champion arose, who clad himself in armour covered with knife blades. Then, armed with a large knife in each hand, he contrived to get himself swallowed by the monster. Once inside he rolled violently about, inflicting mortal intestinal injuries. When the creature expired, he used the large knives to cut himself out and return safely to the outer world. In the Dalry case the legitimate question of how the monster was foolish or insensitive enough to swallow a morsel bristling with knives is ingeniously explained. The champion, the local blacksmith, Michael Fleming, fashioned a coat of armour covered with knife blades, which could be retracted to lie in the interstices so that the White Snake experienced no problems in ingesting him. But once inside all the blades were released to stick up vertically – and painfully. The unnamed knight at Motte of Urr presumably showed the same talent for technological innovation.

It only remains to add that at Dalry a proper concern was displayed for the environment as the locals cut up the remains of the White Snake and dispatched them down the river at the next spate.

Sources

Maxwell, J.H. (pub.)   *Maxwell's Guide Book to the Stewartry of Kirkcudbright,*
    8th edn Castle Douglas, 1908

Trotter, R.   *Lowran Castle* Dumfries, 1822

Trotter, R. de B.   *Galloway Gossip, The Stewartry* Dumfries, 1901

Truckell, A.   *Galloway Folk Lore* in *The Quest, Christmas, 1956*
    Castle Douglas, 1956

THE WITCH WOMAN OF EARLSTOUN

Since Earlstoun tower house was for long the home of one of Galloway's most celebrated families, it would be tactful to assume that its occupancy by a "witch ladye" predated the acquisition of tower and estate by the Gordons in 1601. The lady in question had used her black arts to capture the affections of young laird William, who was already betrothed to the winsome and virtuous Annie from Shirmers south of today's Ken Bridge on the Dalry to Castle Douglas road. The devastating news of her rival's success was revealed to Annie in a dream interpreted to her with brutal candour by one of her attendants:

"…of her wee finger he noo thinks mair
Than the haill of his Annie's hand."

When luckless Annie asked where she might find a wizard powful enough to nullify the witch's spell, help came from an unlikely quarter. Her parrot (popinjay) revealed that he had formerly been the witch's pet during an involuntary sojourn in her tower, in the course of which he had learned the crucial word that undid all her spells. He was despatched with haste to Earlstoun, where he contrived to sing a lament heard by William and his new love as they strolled in the policies. His song of the bonny dove of Shirmars deprived of her mate by the grey owlet caught the attention of William, who asked the source of the "waile of woe". It also alarmed the witch, who tried to bribe the parrot into silence. However the bird insisted on finishing the song by uttering the fateful word which destroyed the witch's spell. In despair the lady rushed off through the woods and hurled herself into the boiling waters of the famous Earlstoun Linn or waterfall (now sadly no more since the Galloway hydro-electric scheme raised the river level.)

The story makes what seems to be its first appearance in 1893 as *The Witch Ladye* in John Nichlson's *Historical and Traditional Tales*, where it is credited to W. M'Lellan but sub-titled *An Ancient Ballad*. It appears again in *The Gallovidian Annual* for 1920, where it is simply described in the latter style. It is certainly tempting to regard it as an authentic, traditional ballad as it contains many of the characteristics of a work of that kind both in form and in content; M'Lellan could have been its collector. On the other hand it could be the work of a Galloway Sir Walter Scott, supplementing the efforts of the composers of traditional ballads, and the name of Allan Cunningham comes uneasily to mind. Whoever the author was, he or she has produced a marvellously eerie and spine-chilling description of the witch's working practices:

"For scho's gather'd witch-dewe in the Kells kirkyard

In the mirke howe of the moone;
And fede hersell with the wilde witche-milke
With a rede-hotte burnynge spoone."

We are on more solid ground in pointing out an interesting parallel in Kirkcolm parish in Wigtownshire. Here also is a story of a bird or birds playing a crucial role in a folk tale by imparting vital information. The story however is not in verbal but in pictorial form, being carved on the fascinating tenth century Kilmorie Cross now in Kirkcolm churchyard after some peregrinations round the parish. Its reverse side probably tells the story of the great Germano-Norse hero Sigurd being warned by birds about a projected attempt on his life. However, to be privy to this information Sigurd had had to learn the language of birds by killing the dragon Fafnir. The uncomplicated Galloway version simply made the bird a parrot and extended its speech competence beyond the repetitive.

Sources

Crossley-Holland, K.   *The Norse Myths* London, 1987
Nicholson, J.   *Historical and Traditional Tales* Kirkcudbright, 1893
Wood, J.M. (ed.)   *The Gallovidian Annual 1920* Dumfries, 1920

THE HOLM OF DALARRAN

The tall, elegant, standing stone that graces the Holm of Dalarran above the Ken Bridge close to the Dalry-Castle Douglas road creates an interface between folklore and archaeology. In the former, the monolith plays a central role in the supernatural tale of the Black Horseman of Dalarran. He is to be seen at the bridge, formerly the ford, where the highway crosses the Garpel Burn. A gigantic, black-haired man clad in black armour on a suitably proportioned black horse, he comes down the burn, goes across the holm to the standing stone, pauses briefly there, then crosses the Ken and ascends the hillside beyond. This alarming manifestation is, unusually, to be witnessed at dawn. The reason for the call at the standing stone is that his mortal remains are (or were) buried there.

Holm of Dalarran standing stone

As for his identity, local tradition obligingly furnishes two candidates. One is the king of the Scots who died in his hour of triumph in a battle against would-be settlers from Ireland (the fact that the Scots originally came from Ireland casts some confusion over this account). The other, more popular, candidate is a Danish king who was allegedly defeated and killed here by a Scottish army in the early ninth century. Tradition affirms that arms and armour from the battle of the reader's choice have been dug up on the holm, including finds close to the standing stone.

Archaeology paints a different, more restrained, but no less fascinating picture. Standing stones, dating from The Bronze Age nearly four thousand years ago, do indeed occasionally have a burial in a stone-lined kist close to them, presumably that of a leader, although obviously not a Scot or a Dane. These sometimes yield grave goods, including bronze swords. In this connection it is worthy of note that when accounts of the weapons found on the holm are at all precise, they mention only one sword; in 1908 this was reportedly in the possession of Mr Spalding, owner of the nearby property of Holm. And so the monument raised in the mists of pre-history over three thousand years ago above the remains of a dead leader may have been the genesis for the traditional Glenkens belief in the awesome Black Horseman of Dalarran.

Sources

Harper, M.	*Rambles in Galloway* Dalbeattie, 1896
M'Kerlie, P.	*History of the Lands and Their Owners in Galloway, Volume Third* Edinburgh, 1877
Maxwell, J. H. (pub.)	*Maxwell's Guide Book to the Stewartry of Kirkcudbright* Castle Douglas, 1908
Trotter, R. de B.	*Galloway Gossip, the Stewartry* Dumfries, 1901

WHO WAS AIKEN-DRUM?

The Brownie of Blednoch by packman-poet William Nicholson of Borgue parish is justly celebrated far beyond the confines of Galloway. One of its many attractions is that the plot of the poem is drawn from folklore. Of this latter Nicholson must have had a profound knowledge, acquired from his mother, who possessed a store of it; from his close contact with country people in the course of his itinerant job; and from his attendance as piper at rural weddings, festivals, and festivities. In fact the poem is a classic example of a brownie tale, a type found widely in folklore; the brownie's English equivalent, the goblin, makes a cameo appearance in John Milton's poem *L'Allegro.* And the name of Nicholson's protagonist, Aiken-drum, is not the invention of the poet either for a character of that name (or nickname?) appears in a well known Scottish children's song.

Aiken-drum (after E. A. Hornel)

As for Aiken-drum, Nicholson's fellow-native of Borgue parish John McTaggart shrewdly remarked,

"Some think they (brownies) are of no supernatural origin, but distressed persons, who were obliged to conceal themselves and wander about during some of the past turbulent ages."

In a Galloway context, and particularly in the immediate geographical context of the poem, two classes of "distressed persons" suggest themselves as historical prototypes for Nicholson's brownie.

Firstly, Aiken-drum may be a fugitive Covenanter, of whom many were to be found in Galloway during the politico-religious troubles of the second half of the seventeenth century. In this connection the description of the Brownie's features is significant:

"'Sauf us!' quoth Jock, 'd'ye see sic een?'
Cries Kate, 'there's a hole where a nose should hae been;
And the mouth's like a gash which a horn had ri'en'".

This description tallies very closely with the features of an alarming-looking mask worn to conceal his identity by the famous preacher Alexander Peden of New Luce. It is now on display in the Museum of Scotland in Edinburgh. Presumably similar masks were worn by several Covenaners on the run; otherwise the point of the exercise would have been lost. The other noteworthy detail is in the account of the Brownie's physical appearance: we are told that "his wauchie (feeble) arms...trailed on the grun' by his taeless feet". This brings to mind the enigmatic Silver Sand of S.R.Crockett's *The Raiders*, whose arms had been distorted by torture at the hands of the episcopalian government. And Aiken-drum's abnormal feet could be the result of a common form of torture practised on suspected Covenanters by means of the infamous "Boot".

However, another possibility is that Aiken-drum was a leper and so compelled to live apart from the rest of society. The description of his misshapen appearance may refer in general terms to the disfiguring effects of that disease and the arrival in their midst of a leper would explain the horrified reaction of the villagers at the start of the poem and their desire instantly to be rid of him. In fact a leper colony once existed in the area at Liberland on the northern border of Wigtownshire about two miles west of Loch Mabery, the source of the River Bladnoch. Traces of the ruins of houses are still to be seen there. A leper desperate for some contact with normal society could well have followed the river valley down to the first sizeable settlement, Kirkcowan, and begged to be allowed tenuous contact with it. (Topographical and other references in the poem make it clear that Kirkcowan is the setting of the poem, Bladnoch referring to the river of that name and not the village.)

The enduring appeal of Aiken-drum and *The Brownie of Blednoch* is demonstrated by the number and range of versions of the story. Just over a hundred years after William Nicholson's *tour de force* Philippa, Lady Galloway, included a fine prose version of the tale in her *Folk Tales of Scotland,* published in 1943. Then in 1951 the story, entitled *Aiken-Drum the Brownie*, appeared in a series of readers for primary schools, the *Janet and John Story Books.* But surely clinching evidence of its universal appeal came in 1960 when Lady Galloway's version appeared in Esperanto, the totally artificial, international language:

"Iun vesperon inter krepusko kaj noktoveno, kiam grizo regis trankvile super la akvoj de la golfo Uigtaun, situanta inter la montetoj Stewartry kaj la marco Cree…"

And the story does not appear only in written forms, however exotic, for the painting *The Brownie o Blednoch* by Kirkcudbright artist E.A. Hornel hangs in Glasgow's Kelvingrove Gallery. It also appears as an illustration to the poem in Malcolm Harper's *Bards of Galloway;* it would be interesting to know whether Harper persuaded his friend Hornel to paint the picture specially for the poetry collection. Glasgow's premier art gallery and the universal language Esperanto are a long way from the simple world of packman William Nicholson.

Sources

Harper, M.	*The Poetical Works of William Nicholson* Dalbeattie, 1897
Whiteford, J.	personal communication

GALLOWAY GALOSHANS

Galoshans (the name has several variants) is the Scottish version of a folk play of great antiquity with roots going back to the Middle Ages. Found in all four countries of the United Kingdom, it has waxed and waned in popularity over the centuries with a peak in the late nineteen hundreds followed by an abrupt, terminal decline so that by the 1920s the custom survived only in a few rural areas. These included Whithorn and the Port William district. By 1992 the sole performance of galoshans was in Biggar. However, the contemporary practice of young people dressing up and visiting houses at Hallowe'en to sing or recite and receive in return gifts of sweets, fruit, and money is a relic of the galoshans tradition.

The galoshans play was very simple. After a short introduction two characters fought with wooden swords until one was killed. A request was then made for a doctor and answered invariably by Doctor Brown, who, with the aid of the contents of a bottle, miraculously restored the dead duellist. The two antagonists were reconciled and the play ended with an appeal for donations of money. Speeches were in verse and occasionally sung, the words showing a remarkable similarity all over Scotland. Each generation tended to add topical allusions in the manner of a pantomime and these allow the various versions to be dated. The core cast of four was augmented by a variable number of guisers, often representing historical figures or contemporary celebrities, and restricted to walk-on roles.

In a letter to Sir Herbert Maxwell of Monreith in 1931, the noted antiquary James Curle suggested that the two duellists in the play were St George of Cappadocia and a Galatian (hence the play's name) since the saint was slain by a man of that race. He considered that the King George of Maxwell's version was in fact the holy man. However, another theory claims the name of the play comes from an old French word "galocher", to play the clown, which came to England with the Norman Conquest and found its way to Scotland two centuries later.

The first mention of a Galloway performance of galoshans is in McTaggart's *Scottish Gallovidian Encyclopaedia* of 1824, and presumably refers to the Borgue area. By the play's late nineteenth century heyday it was being performed at five other locations in the Ken-Dee valley: Kirkcudbright, Castle Douglas, Clarebrand, Laurieston, and Balmaghie parish, as well as two unidentified locations. For one of the latter a drawing of a performance exists. Across the Cree in Wigtownshire the only places where performances are known to have taken place are Whithorn, the Port William area (assuming Sir Herbert Maxwell collected his version locally), and another unidentified location in the South Machars. At two places galoshans was performed at Christmas-New Year but in all the rest it took place at Hallowe'en. Strangely enough, in none of the Galloway examples was the word galoshans used. In one unidentified Stewartry location the custom was known as White Boys while McTaggart calls it Yule-Boys, the former name referring to the borrowed parental white shirts or gowns traditionally worn by the players.

The Galloway versions of the play exhibit interesting variations frequently involving in the Stewartry the discovery by one duellist that he had killed a close relative, different in every location and most unexpectedly at Clarebrand "my father's only son".   At Port William a sneering reference to one duellist as "a poor silly boy driving St Patrick's sheep" may be an echo of the antagonism felt in the nineteenth century towards Irish immigrants, a feeling made very clear in *The New Statistical Account* reports for some South Machars parishes.

At Whithorn, W.R.I. members recalled in the 1970s having seen the play performed in their earlier years. And well known author John McNeillie (Ian S. Niall) reported in his *Country Life* column that his father used to reminisce about visits from groups of actors at Hallowe'en in various South Machars locations where the family lived . He himself had a very early childhood memory of such a visit to his grandfather's farm at South Clutag and the merriment it engendered:

"Hallowe'en, Hallowe'en comes but once a year,
  And when it comes we hope to give all good cheer".

In at least one case that hope was obviously realised.

Sources

Curle, J.	unpublished letter to Sir Herbert Maxwell
Gregor, Dr W.	*Folklore in Galloway* in Annual Report of the British Association 1897 London, 1897
Hayward, B.	*Galoshins; The Scottish Folk Play* Edinburgh, 1992.
McTaggart, J.	*The Scottish Gallovidian Encyclopaedia; new edn* Perthshire, 1981
Maxwell, Sir H.	unpublished MS
Vance, Mrs. C.	unpublished MS

ROWANS, BORT STONES, AND ADDERHEADS

Since witches have been a prominent feature of this section on folk lore, it seems only prudent to list some charms designed to ward off their malign influence. The first type was in the mineral category and consisted of perforated discs of shale or cannel coal known as bort stones, hag stones, or mare stones. Equally efficacious was a holt stone, a pebble with a natural hole. Both versions protected horses and cattle from witches if placed above a byre- or stable door on the inside. Alternatively they could be rubbed over cattle or kept in a watering trough, the latter being the method adopted at the farm of Garchew north of Newton Stewart More difficult to obtain was the clear stone known as an adder bead or adderhead, allegedly created on midsummer's eve by adders, whose hissing and blowing engendered a froth which passed over the animal's body and came off at the tail metamorphosed into a mineral. Another version, no more credible, claims an adder stone was the result of a co-operative venture on the part of thirteen adders. However created, the end product certainly exists: an adder bead from Glenluce is in the possession of the National Museum of Scotland.

Reassuringly mundane and seemingly equally effective as an anti-witch charm was a used horseshoe nailed over a stable- or byre door. Writing in 1900, a local minister recorded that there were as many horseshoes above doors in his parish as there were families but had no explanation to offer for the superstition. Perhaps his parishioners did not wish to hurt his feelings by admitting they had taken out additional insurance against the forces of evil.

However, the most popular charm by far was in the vegetable category: the wood of the rowan tree, deployed in a myriad of different forms from a tree planted "Wi' its airm across the (house) door" through pieces of wood on the mantelpiece or over the byre door and twigs woven into the tails of cattle to timber from the tree incorporated into the furnishings of house or byre. With young women wearing strings of rowan berries and fishermen using thole pins of rowan wood, the mischief-making opportunities for witches should have been discouragingly limited. And the rowan weapon was deployed right across Galloway from Kirkmaiden and Port Logan in the west by way of Borgue, Rerrick, Balmaghie, and Kells to Corsock in the east. Yet we remember uneasily the ending of Violet Jacob's memorable poem *The Rowan:*

> "… I feel the lang een set
> Like a doom upon my heid,
> For the warlock's livin' yet –
> *But the rowan's deid!"*

<u>Sources</u>

Bell, T.   *Galloway Superstitions* <u>in</u> *The Gallovidian Annual 1939*
                             Dumfries, 1939

Glover, J.   *Galloway Folk-Lore* <u>in</u> *The Gallovidian, Autumn 1906*
                             Dumfries, 1906

Gregor, Dr W.   *Folklore in Galloway* <u>in</u> *Annual Report of the British
                             Association 1897* London, 1897

"Herd, A Galloway"   *About Galloway Folk* Castle Douglas, 1900

Wood, J. M.   *Witchcraft and Superstitious Record in South-West Scotland*
                             Dumfries, 1911

THE REAL SIR PATRICK SPENS?

The traditional Scottish ballads could arguably be regarded as the tabloid newspapers of their day, the fourteenth to the end of the seventeenth century. Both are intended for an unsophisticated, popular market and both narrate sensational events: conflicts, major crimes, tragedies, with a particular preference for the involvement of well known names. The narrative style matches the sensationalism of the content with emphasis on sanguinary details. Factual fidelity is not a notable feature. In the case of the ballads the latter tendency is exacerbated by the reality of oral transmission for several hundred years with the consequent "Chinese Whispers" syndrome. It can therefore be difficult to identify the historical event which led to the creation of a ballad.

This is certainly true of one of the best known ballads, *Sir Patrick Spens*. Various candidates have been put forward for the royal princess requiring transportation between Scotland and Scandinavia; no trace in historical records of the eponymous hero has been found. However a plausible theory suggests the real person behind the ballad was a prominent Scottish nobleman from Barnbarroch estate south-west of Wigtown by name of Sir Patrick Vaus – and some would say 50% accuracy in the name is very reasonable in tabloid-style reporting. Sir Patrick, although with no seafaring connection, was certainly a leading figure at the court of King James VI. A churchman (at least nominally), well educated, and well connected, he was made a Senator of the College of Justice, that is a judge, in 1576 and six years later received a knighthood. After four more years he became one of the king's closest advisers as a member of the Privy Council.

Then came the event which may link the laird of Barnbarroch to the famous ballad. In 1587 he was sent with another ambassador to Denmark to negotiate King James's marriage to one (apparently any one) of the daughters of the King of Denmark. Preliminary negotiations must have gone well for on returning to Scotland the two ambassadors were congratulated on having "trewlie honnestlie and diligentlie" performed their charge. The praise was merited for in the summer of 1589 a marriage between James VI and Princess Anne of Denmark was agreed on and the bride set off for Scotland and matrimony. However her fleet was severely buffeted by a gale and forced to seek shelter in Norway, where she remained. Revealing an unexpected romantic streak, James then resolved to join his bride in Scandinavia despite the advanced season and summoned Sir Patrick and other courtiers to attend him. Their late October departure was attended by severe weather and much resulting national anxiety. Continuing gales forced them back to lie off St Monans in Fife until the weather improved. However, the voyage was eventually accomplished and the marriage solemnized in Norway. For some reason Sir Patrick returned in December some months before the happy couple.

The above sequence of events with their accompanying climate of anxiety and undoubtedly rumour and inevitable misinformation perhaps gives the historical background for *Sir Patrick Spens*. The Galloway courtier and diplomat has become a ship's captain but this is the tabloid world. And it may be that Sir Patrick does make a cameo appearance as his rightful self in the person of "the eldern knight, sat at the King's right knee" who recommends the unfortunate ship's master for the voyage. And the historical prototype of the latter? Taking the attendant confusion into account, he might conceivably be John Gardiner, master of the *Lion* of Leith, who was paid one thousand pounds Scots for conveying Vaus and his fellow ambassador to Denmark in August, 1587.

If the identification of Spens as Vaus is correct, then the ballad contains a delightful irony. In it Sir Patrick impetuously decides to return to Scotland after being accused of freeloading at the Danish court. In real life, in 1589 in anticipation of his bride's arrival with her retinue, the king wrote to Barnbarroch's Sir Patrick instructing him to send to Holyrood the maximum possible quantities of beef and mutton on the hoof together with wildfowl, venison, and "uther stuff meit for this purpois" so that the Danish guests could receive appropriate hospitality. In the matter of freeloading the laird of Barnbarroch was to be victim not guilty party.

Sources

Anon.   *Sir Patrick Spens* <u>in</u> *The Gallovidian Annual, 1924*
                                   Dumfries, 1924

Henderson, T.   *Scottish Vernacular Literature —*

Vans Agnew, R.   *Correspondence of Sir Patrick Waus of Barnbarroch* Edinburgh,
                                   1887

Built in 1780 probably on the site of Sir Patrick Vaus's residence, Barnbarroch mansion burned down in 1941.

MURDER MOST FOUL

DARK DEEDS AT GLENLUCE ABBEY

As the Reformation in Scotland grew imminent in the mid-sixteenth century, the rich lands held by the church attracted the keen and acquisitive interest of the lairds. Here in Galloway the fertile acres of Glenluce Abbey in the valley of the River Luce were coveted by two prominent landowners, Sir John Gordon of Lochinvar in the Glenkens and Gilbert Kennedy, Earl of Cassilis, in south Ayrshire. The former enjoyed the advantage of being related to the abbot and in consequence in 1557 received from the latter a feu charter granting him all the abbey lands. To secure his position Gordon took possession of the abbey itself and quartered there a force of armed retainers. However there then appeared out of the blue one Thomas Hay from Aberdeenshire, who succeeded in persuading Queen Mary and her then husband, King Francis of France, to petition the pope, successfully, for him to be appointed abbot at Glenluce. If he was not then in league with Cassilis he soon afterwards was for he and his retinue stayed with Cassilis at Maybole while a reluctant Gordon was eased out of the abbey.

Cassilis was well and speedily rewarded for his hospitality: within a month of his installation as abbot, Hay granted to his former host a feu charter of the abbey lands. The traditional version claims that Hay inconveniently died before all the transfer documents were complete, that the resourceful Cassilis had the necessary papers forged by a helpful monk, and then had the forger murdered to ensure his silence. To tie up any loose ends he had the murderer, Carnochan, framed for theft and hanged. However, the truth seems to be that Cassilis did not require such drastic expedients. The historian J.M. Rusk discovered a second charter of twelve years later also signed by a still surviving Thomas. This second document conveyed to Cassilis the few abbey assets carelessly omitted from the previous charter.

Thomas Hay's generosity with church property did not go unrewarded. A grateful Cassilis granted to him and his family the part of the former abbey lands known as Park, where they built themselves a new residence, Castle of Park, still a prominent feature of the local landscape and now restored as a dwelling house. Another popular local tradition, that Castle of Park was built of stone recycled from the abbey, is incorrect for the latter was, according to Robert Heron, "almost entire" in 1646, over 50 years after the neighbouring castle was built. Descendants of Thomas Hay held the Park estate, latterly combined with neighbouring Dunragit, until 1875.

As for Gilbert, Earl of Cassilis, he has many misdeeds to his account but the murders of an unnamed forger-monk and a hit-man by the name of Carnochan do not appear to be among them.

Sources

M'Kerlie, P   *History of the Lands and Their Owners in Galloway; new edition* vol. I Paisley, 1906

Rusk, J.   *History of The Parish and Abbey of Glenluce* Edinburgh, 1930

FOUL PLAY ON THE PORT WILLIAM ROAD

The killings traditionally associated with Glenluce Abbey and Gilbert Kennedy may have little basis in fact but no doubts can be entertained about two murders which took place in the space of two months in 1880 in the Glenluce district to the great alarm of the residents.

The first has unhappily familiar, contemporary overtones for it seems to have been drink-related and the time of the event and age of the victim would be familiar to any modern criminologist. One April Saturday evening around eleven o'clock a group of farmservants, four men and a girl, the men apparently well under the influence of alcohol, left Glenluce to walk home by the Auchenmalg-Port William road armed with a "carry-out". It is difficult to establish the sequence of events for the evidence is confused and contradictory but it seems that two of the group, James Dunning and Thomas Murray, dropped behind the others at the Barlockhart roadend. The remaining two men, John Ramsay and Robert Haney, were in fractious mood and so Mary Murray, Thomas's sister, left them just beyond the farm of Barnsallie and proceeded on her own.

Milton smithy near Barnsallie in 1880

From then on the picture is even more muddied. It appears that Ramsay and Haney may have lain down by the roadside to sleep just after Mary Murray's departure while behind them Dunning and Murray came on separately from the Barlockhart roadend.

Whether and in what circumstances any of them joined up again is impossible to ascertain with any certainty. Some time later Haney arrived in an agitated state at Milton smithy a hundred yards up the road to Whitefield Loch . He said that he had awoken from his roadside sleep to see a short distance away Ramsay crawling on his hands and knees as he tried unsuccessfully to get to his feet. When Haney went over to him, he discovered Ramsay had sustained a horrific wound to the head and was semi-conscious and unable to speak. While Mr McHarrie, the blacksmith, hurried to attend to the injured man, Haney hastened back to Glenluce to summon the local doctor, Dr McCormack. However, the victim, who was eighteen years old, died before medical help arrived.

A search revealed a spade covered with blood and hair outside McHarrie's door. This, the murder weapon, had been carried by the victim when he left Glenluce. In his statement to the police Dunning said he had found it lying on the road and had left it at the door of the nearest house, the blacksmith's. Next morning the police arrested Dunning, an assistant dairyman at nearby Kilfillan farm. The fact that he was found in bed wearing a pair of bloodstained trousers did nothing to allay the suspicions of the constabulary.

In August Dunning stood trial at the autumn assizes in Dumfries before Lord Mure. At the conclusion of the two-day proceedings the jury, clearly unimpressed by the prosecution case, took only six minutes to return a not guilty verdict. They were perhaps mindful of a defence claim that Ramsay's bloodstained hat had been recovered from Haney's house. Their decision was greeted by loud, and swiftly suppressed, cheering in court, which was replicated by a large crowd outside when Dunning emerged. That public opinion emphatically agreed with the jury was confirmed when the acquitted man returned by train to Glenluce. The verdict had been telegraphed ahead of him and the train was greeted by cheering crowds at Newton Stewart and Kirkcowan stations with a climactic, enormous, and enthusiastic throng at Glenluce itself.

It is doubtful if the Ramsay family shared in the general enthusiasm for no one had been found guilty of their son's murder. That may be the reason why local people decided to have a trial of their own of an unconventional kind. They agreed with the Advocate Depute's statement at the proceedings in Dumfries that the murderer was one of three men, presumably Dunning, Haney, or Murray, and so three trees of the same species were planted at the roadside where the murder had occurred, each representing one of the three prime suspects. It was confidently predicted that the trees representing the two innocent parties would soon wither and die, thus eliminating the men they stood for from the enquiry. The prediction appears to have been realised for today at the murder spot one solitary tree stands at the roadside on the west side of the highway. Unfortunately local tradition is unable to supply the name of the man whose guilt was thus made so manifest to the world. However, the mute witness perhaps justifies the confidence expressed by local schoolmaster John A. McKemmie in a poem written soon after the murder. The dominie considered the truth of the affair would out, not necessarily through the judicial process:

"I passed the place where Ramsey fell
And weltered in his blood.
Who did this crime but one can tell
Twas He that caused the Flood.
He brings the darkest deeds to light,
And needs no human aid;
Against our God he need not fight
The man that used the spade."

All that can be added is that Haney eventually left the area to live with his married son at the picturesquely named Teapot Cottage on the hill road from Creetown to Gatehouse by way of Gatehouse station, where he displayed no inclination to enlarge his circle of acquaintances.

Sources

The Ayr Advertiser	issue of 8th April, 1880
Glen of Luce W.R.I.	personal communications from various members
Higgins, Mrs. K.	personal communication
Harper, Mrs. I.	personal communication
McQuaker, J.	unpublished papers
Wigtownshre Free Press	issue of 2nd September, 1880

THE CROWN INN AFFAIR

Barely had the shock waves created by the Barnsallie slaying begun to subside than the Glenluce area was improbably the scene of another murder, this time in the village itself. The victim was James Milligan, native of Kirkcowan and licensee of the Crown Inn (now the Commercial Inn) halfway down the hill on the left-hand side in Glenluce main street. In the early hours of the morning of the 3rd of June, 1880, an unknown person entered the Crown Inn, apparently bent on robbery. Milligan was known to keep a substantial sum of money in an upstairs room: when asked to change a five pound banknote (a large amount in the late nineteenth century) he invariably went to the first floor for the necessary money. Indications were that the thief had gone upstairs to this room but had found it locked and was unable to gain entry. He then seemingly returned downstairs and entered Milligan's bedroom presumably in search of his keys. The landlord awoke and a struggle ensued during which the unfortunate innkeeper was fatally injured. His elderly housekeeper, Mrs McCreadie, disturbed by the struggle, went to investigate and was attacked in her turn to her serious injury. The burglar then made his escape by the back door, taking with him only a gold watch and chain from Milligan's bedroom.

The Crown Inn, Glenluce, in 1880

On starting their investigations into the crime, the police found they had two witnesses, both of whom had been resident in the inn. Although Mrs McCreadie, the housekeeper, eventually made a full recovery she was unable to give a coherent account of what had happened or supply any details about the intruder. The investigators obtained equally little help from the other witness, Mary Anderson, Milligan's maidservant. In her evidence she said she was awakened by the sound of a violent struggle, took fearful refuge beneath her bed, and emerged only when she heard the back door close.

However, several promising clues were available. It was reasonably felt that the criminal must be local for only locals knew Mr Milligan's financial arrangements (£100 in banknotes was discovered in the untouched upstairs room). The maid, Mary Anderson, had heard a spring-cart pass just as the clock struck two, as had other villagers. An auger stolen with other tools (including the murder weapon, an axe,) about midnight from the joiner's shop at Drumflower, five miles to the west, was found upstairs at the Crown. Also found in the same location was a hat presumably the property of the murderer. And the latter had removed his boots before entering the property, leaving in consequence two imprints of his stockinged feet on the whitened flagstones of the inn's ground floor passageway.

Suspects too were not unplentiful, the result of a widely spread dragnet. A suspicious-looking individual had been observed washing spots of blood from his clothing at distant Carronbridge north of Thornhill in Dumfriesshire. And in those politically incorrect times all tramps in the area were automatically under suspicion. Also under scrutiny were two men with local connections, who claimed to have been in Ayrshire on the night of the murder. And certain inconsistencies in the story given by Mary Anderson attracted attention and caused speculation about a possible boyfriend who might have been the guilty party.

National publicity was not wanting. The then *Glasgow Herald* dispatched to Glenluce a "special correspondent", whose subsequent report, in highly emotive language with a wealth of evocative detail, would have been a credit to a reporter from a modern-day "Red Top". Perhaps under this journalistic stimulus, the investigation at first proceeded rapidly. All tramps in Galloway were questioned…and cleared. The bloodstained Carronbridge suspect was similarly eliminated while the Ayshire duo produced a satisfactory alibi. More positive was the discovery that the murderer's hat from the crime scene had been sold in a Glenluce shop a year previously. The offer by the government of a £100 reward led to such anticipation of an imminent arrest that for a few days crowds met every train at Glenluce station in expectation of seeing the criminal returning under escort.

But then the trail went cold. A Scotland Yard detective was called in to assist at the beginning of July but to no avail. By November dissatisfied Glenluce residents petitioned the Wigtownshire Police Committee, complaining that no arrest had been made and asking for a police report on the investigation. They were assured that all leads had been followed up but without result. Local bard J.A. McKemmie was driven to take up his pen once more but this time in sardonic vein:

" Even now, if you should slay a publican-
  Burn homes – missionaries – kill a common man –
  Flee to Glenluce; law will not reach you there,
  Unless, worse luck, you should have bagged a hare,
  Then Law's dread myrmidons are on your track".

And there the matter has remained but for one tantalising development. Eleven years after the murder, in June, 1891, a farm worker was repairing a turf dyke on the farm of Auchtralure just to the south-west of Stranraer. Hidden in it he found a dirty, gold watch, which had clearly been in the ground for a long time. Because of its poor condition he sold it for a few pence and after passing through several hands it was optimistically handed in for repair to a Newton Stewart jeweller. He at once recognised it as the watch stolen from the Crown Inn eleven years before: a description had been circulated to all jewellers at the time. The discovery re-focused attention on the maid, Mary Anderson, and her hypothetical boyfriend. By this time Mary had emigrated to America but people remembered that before doing so she had lived for some time in the Backrampart district on the west side of Stranraer. There was animated speculation as to what number would be achieved if two and two were added together...

Sources

Ayr Advertiser	issue of 10th June, 1880
Higgins, Mrs. K.	personal communication
Wigtownshire Free Press	various issues of 1880 and 1891

NAMES TO RECKON WITH

GALLOWAY'S *TITANIC* SURVIVOR

Galloway has a well known connection with the *Titanic* disaster through First Officer William Murdoch of Dalbeattie, who was in charge of the ship when she hit the iceberg and whose very rapid and appropriate response has been insufficiently acknowledged. Less well known is the local link with a notable *Titanic* survivor, Junior Wireless Operator Harold Bride. Bride was not Galloway-born (he came from Kent) and his association with the area began after the tragedy and during the First World War, but he married a Wigtownshire girl and the county became his home for over thirty years.

Bride, 22 years old in 1912, played a significant role in the actual disaster and a prominent one in the creation of the *Titanic* legend. Having taken over the watch from Senior Operator Phillips at midnight, he was on duty when the ship struck the iceberg. Although Phillips at once resumed his station, Bride made a historic contribution to maritime radio. At his suggestion Phillips switched from transmitting the regular CQD distress call to the newly introduced SOS, the first transmission of that famous signal ("It may be the last chance we get," Bride had remarked with gallows humour). And Bride went back and forward between the radio shack and the bridge with incoming messages from ships in the area. Furthermore the position of the radio cabin close to the bridge on the boat deck gave the Junior Wireless Operator a grandstand view of the unfolding tragedy.

Bride and Phillips stayed on at their post even after Captain Smith personally instructed them to leave:

"You can do no more. Abandon your cabin. Now it's every man for himself. You look out for yourselves. I release you."

It was then that a dramatic event occurred when a stoker entered the radio room and tried to wrest Phillips's lifejacket from him. Bride gave varying accounts of what happened next but in one he was quite unequivocal:

"I did my duty. I hope I finished him. I don't know. We left him on the cabin floor and he was not moving."

With power failing and the ship about to sink, the two men finally went out on deck, where Bride helped to launch a collapsible lifeboat from the roof of the officers' quarters close by. He was swept overboard with it, trapped under it as it capsized, and freed himself only with difficulty. After swimming around for some time he was hauled on board the overturned and overcrowded boat, receiving permanent injuries when his feet became jammed between slats and someone sat on them. At dawn the surviving complement of the overturned boat were taken on board a ship's lifeboat and later transferred to the rescue ship *Carpathia*.

Harold Bride in 1912

But Harold Bride's part in the *Titanic* story was far from over. In spite of his crushed feet and frostbite, he assisted the *Carpathia*'s sole radio operator in his duties for the three days it took the vessel to reach New York. One of the enduring images of the disaster is of Harold Bride, both legs bandaged, being carried off the *Carpathia* when she docked. Then, thanks to the business acumen of his boss, Signor Marconi (for the wireless operators were employed by that firm, not by the shipping line), Bride's account of the disaster was the first full version to reach the press, the *New York Times*, no less. And that account established some of the most famous elements in the *Titanic* legend, like Phillips's dedication and the ship's band playing as the vessel went down.

The various courts of enquiry also heightened Bride's profile as his radio cabin vantage point made him a vital witness to the ship's last hours.

Then, according to one historian, "Bride left the Marconi Company and disappeared." In fact, he disappeared to Stranraer in the following way. Clearly Marconi did not make their most famous employee redundant; they had given him a gold watch to commemorate his part in the transmission of the world's first SOS. But with his damaged feet Bride would not have passed the compulsory medical examinations for liner crews introduced after the *Titanic* disaster. He was therefore sent to train White Star wireless operators at the company's Liverpool training school. However a shore job did not appeal to Bride and so he joined a shipping line operating in the Irish Sea, where no medicals were required. With the First World War now raging, he was eagerly accepted and joined the *Mona's Isle*, which was then requisitioned by the Admiralty as an anti-submarine net layer and in that capacity came to Stranraer. There Bride met local schoolteacher Lucy Downie at a canteen for servicemen and auxiliaries staffed by local volunteers. Romance flourished and the couple married in 1920, when the *Titanic* survivor left the sea at his wife's insistence and made his home in Stranraer.

Sadly the happy ending which Harold Bride surely deserved does not seem to have occurred. For the next twenty years the couple lived at several addresses in Stranraer and its neighbourhood with Bride apparently in the pharmaceutical field and variously described as "company director", owner of chemist's shop, representative for a pharmaceutical firm, and "commercial traveller". The hint that times were financially difficult seems substantiated by the fact that, very unusually for the period, Lucy Bride was back teaching a year after the couple's first child was born.

Around the start of the Second World War the family left the area for Tayside but returned in 1949 to take the tenancy of Glasserton manse outside Whithorn. The next year Mrs Bride joined the staff of Whithorn school primary dept. Her husband had apparently retired: he told at least one Whithorn resident he had been able to do so after receiving a bequest from a lady whose life he had saved on the *Titanic*. (This may have been the lady whom Bride and Phillips found in a near-fainting condition near their wireless cabin in the ship's last hours and revived with the aid of a chair and a glass of water.) And now the former wireless operator found a way of life congenial to him. He was a frequent visitor to Alex McGhie's radio shop in Whithorn and spent a great deal of time at the Decca Navigation Station at nearby Kidsdale. This sent out a high frequency radio signal which helped ships in the North Atlantic to plot their position accurately. An operator there remembered the quiet, little man who came in and stayed for hours, often eating a packed lunch, while he listened to and watched the business of the station. He did not mention his *Titanic* connection there but some of his Whithorn acquaintances knew of it.

The pleasant Glasserton interlude lastly only till 1955, when Mrs Bride left Whithorn school and the Brides moved to Prestwick and then, seemingly, to East Kilbride, for Harold Bride is buried there, having died in Springburn Hospital in 1956. But the abiding memory is perhaps of him at Kidsdale radio station in the early 1950's. One wonders what thoughts were going through his mind then as he sat once again listening to radio signals relating to shipping in the North Atlantic. Surely he must have been remembering other traffic of that kind on the terrible, momentous night forty years before when the unthinkable happened and the "unsinkable" *Titanic* went to her doom. He certainly could never have anticipated the last, extraordinary chapter in the extraordinary story, which occurred late in 2005 when, thanks to the miracle of robot submersibles and their cameras, TV viewers saw the interior of the radio cabin on the *Titanic,* the first human sight of it since Bride and Phillips walked out (after carefully switching off the power, as the images proved) just before the great liner sank that cold April night over ninety years ago.

Sources

Davie, M.	*The "Titanic"; The Full Story of a Tragedy* London, 1986
Galloway Gazette	issue of June, 13th, 1970
Gracie, Col. A.	*"Titanic"* Stroud, 1998
Graham, A	personal communication
Lawrie, A.	personal communication
McColm, J.	personal communication
McGhie, A.	personal communication
Mowbray, J. (ed.)	*Sinking of the "Titanic"; Eyewitness Accounts* New York, 1998
Nelson, D.	personal communication
Nelson, Ms. H.	personal communication
Wigtownshire County Council	various valuation rolls
Wilson, J.	personal communication

ONE OF THE FEW

Among the fighter pilots who fought and won the Battle of Britain in 1940 was Sergeant Pilot Andrew McDowall of Milldriggan Mill just outside Kirkinner in Wigtownshire. The McDowall family were famous millers, who had plied their trade in Milldriggan for generations, but Andrew sought a career elsewhere, as an engineer on Clydeside. He also joined the RAFVR and became a pilot.

In June, 1939, just before the outbreak of the Second World War, he transferred from the RAFVR to become a full-time flier with the famous 602 (City of Glasgow) Squadron of the RAF as one of four sergeant-pilots. When circumstances found him flying over his home area, he would land close to Milldriggan in a field with a pronounced slope in order to join his thoroughly alarmed parents for a cup of tea. If time did not permit a landing, he would fly disconcertingly low over the house and drop a message in a shell case.

On the outbreak of war in September, 1939, the squadron moved to Drem airfield near North Berwick in East Lothian and it was from there that McDowall shot down his first enemy aircraft. Leave was spent back at Milldriggan, often with friends from the squadron, a favourite pastime being poaching wildfowl on one of the neighbouring estates, sometimes (unsportingly) with the aid of an automatic weapon "borrowed" from the resources of the RAF.

Fortunately for the local fauna the squadron was moved south in August, 1940, with the onset of the Battle of Britain, being based at RAF Westhamprett, a satellite station of Tangmere, one of the airfields at the heart of the conflict. After notable service in the fiercest days of the battle, McDowall really came into his own in its latter stages when small numbers of German fighters were sent across the Channel on nuisance raids. At heart an individualist, the sergeant pilot was in his element in the solo patrolling and dogfighting of this time. His reputation as the toughest man in 602 Squadron was cemented when he attacked five German Messerschmitts only to discover that his guns were not working. With his plane and himself badly shot up, he nevertheless managed to make an emergency landing and limp away from it. As soon as he recovered, he set out across the Channel to even the score and returned contented.

Unsurprisingly his contribution to the events of that summer earned "Mac" the DFM and Bar as well as a commission. The latter he initially turned down on the grounds that he could not afford the expense involved. Finally his CO said that if McDowall would agree to be commissioned the squadron would take care of the expense. The offer was accepted and the Milldriggan man ended the war as a Wing Commander and CO of

616 Squadron, the RAF's first jet fighter squadron, equipped with Gloster Meteors. After the war he was for a time a test pilot with Rolls Royce before ending his flying career in civil aviation in South America, a long way in every sense from Kirkinner.

Perhaps the single incident that best sums up Andrew McDowall's qualities as a pilot occurred in late September, 1940. By now the bombers of the Luftwaffe had mainly switched to night raids and 602 Squadron after some hasty training was assigned the task of intercepting the nocturnal intruders. Most of the pilots failed to make any contact with the enemy, the exception being McDowall, who showed an uncanny ability to detect potential targets. He made several sightings and twice opened fire on enemy bombers but because the engagements were over the Channel and the conclusions therefore unrecorded he was unable to claim any kills.

However things were very different when a small force of hostile aircraft attempted to bomb the squadron's base, RAF Westhamprett. Alarmed observers on the ground were watching the imminent raid courtesy of bright moonlight when McDowall's Spitfire appeared from the opposite direction and launched a highly risky head-on attack on the bombers. The leading aircraft was hit, burst into flames, and crashed just beyond the airfield perimeter while its fellows turned tail and fled. McDowall's daring solo action earned him a Bar to his DFC and increased the almost superstitious regard for his nightfighting skills. Perhaps his poaching forays from Milldriggan had not been entirely without benefit.

Sources

Cameron, D.	*Glasgow's Own, 1987*
Donaldson, C.	personal communication
McKie, Mrs. M.	personal communication
Nancarrow, F.	*Glasgow's Fighter Squadron* London, 1942

A STEWARTRY GODMOTHER

The name Meg Callander of Dundrennan was to her contemporaries most definitely one to be reckoned with. That she was notoriously quarrelsome and had a violent temper were the least of the reasons for it was universally considered that she was a witch, indeed the godmother of all her sisters who resided in the Ken-Dee valley from the confluence of the Deugh and the Ken to Meikle Ross headland at the entrance to Kirkcudbright Bay. It was further believed that she held convocations of her subordinates in a large moss close to Gullathole farm, where she lived. And so there was no deep sorrow when at the close of the eighteenth century she died, an octogenarian, appropriately at Hallowe'en. The fact that the night in question was one of violent storm with all the corn stooks and even peat stacks in the countryside blown down was felt to confirm Meg's true nature.

However, Meg's unfortunate husband, John M'Glashan, a quiet and inoffensive man, was well enough liked and so the next evening his neighbour William M'Burnie, an elder, went to spend some time with him and offer any spiritual assistance that might be required. M'Glashan indicated that the previous night had been a traumatic one but furnished no details. Consequently M'Burnie felt morally obliged to stay with him until morning. After an uneventful vigil, he then returned home to be greeted by a wife in an aroused and indignant state. Mrs M'Burnie informed her astonished husband that while he had been keeping M'Glashan company, she had been forced to entertain M'Glashan's deceased wife, Meg Callander. The latter lady had unexpectedly arrived between ten and eleven the previous night "in her deed claes", had seated herself companionably by the fire, and remained there until the cock crew. Then she had emitted an unearthly yell, grabbed her hostess's mutch from her head, tucked it under her left arm, and disappeared out the door at a great rate.

A puzzled and doubtless slightly sceptical M'Burnie returned to Gullathole to check the veracity of his wife's account. When he examined Meg Callander's corpse laid out in the bedroom, he discovered under its left armpit Mrs M'Burnie's mutch...

Sources

Drylie, J.   *Worthies of Dumfriesshire and Galloway* Dumfries, 1908

KIRKCUDBRIGHT'S FORGOTTEN EMPIRE BUILDER

As his name makes clear, Thomas Dunbar Hamilton Douglas, 5th Earl of Selkirk, was related to some of Scotland's most powerful families. Even so, his rise to the earldom was remarkable for he was the seventh son of the family yet succeeded to the title at the age of 28 in consequence of the ravages of ill health on his brothers. In addition to his distinguished relatives, he was acquainted, albeit fleetingly, with two of Scotland's best known names. At the age of seven he was at the family home, St Mary's Isle outside Kirkcudbright, when it was raided in 1778 by Paul Jones's men intent on kidnapping his fortunately absent father. And he was very probably in residence there when Burns visited in 1793 at the invitation of Thomas's eldest brother, Basil, Lord Daer.

The fact that for long his succession to the earldom seemed impossible allowed him to follow a wider range of interests than would have been permitted the heir. Thus a period at Edinburgh University and acquaintance with some of the luminaries of the Enlightenment was followed by a tour of the Highlands, where he witnessed the social consequences of the Clearances. This was a seminal experience, leading him to develop a belief in emigration to British possessions for dispossessed Highlanders (and Irish refugees from the constant unrest in that island) as a measure beneficial both to the emigrants and to the nation if the resulting settlements were located in strategically important locations. His succession to the deceptively named earldom (no connection with the town or county) gave him the influence and wealth to pursue his vision.

The country chosen for his ventures was Canada and in total he established three settlements there over a period of ten years. He was no armchair or academic coloniser for to the practical agricultural experience gained on the farm near Kirkcudbright leased from his father he added extensive travels in existing colonies along the St Lawrence His first attempt, in 1803, was undemandingly successful for it was located in a very accessible position on Prince Edward Island on the Gulf of St Lawrence close to Nova Scotia in a well established area of colonization.

However, things were very different in 1804 with his second settlement, called Baldoon after the family's Wigtownshire estate, their first landholding in Galloway. It was located in Upper Canada, a much more thinly settled and remote area, between Lake Erie and Lake Huron on the shores of Lake St Clair. The choice of location was heavily influenced by the strategic aim of blocking any move eastwards between the former two lakes by American settlers. While the land chosen looked promising, it was in fact susceptible to flooding and malaria. But what really ensured Baldoon's failure was Selkirk's great weakness, faulty judgement of character. After the first outbreak of illness he ordered his governor, Alexander McDonell to move the settlement to higher ground. McDonell's delay in doing so meant that the settlers suffered a second malaria epidemic with fatalities. This effectively put an end to Baldoon although the survivors moved to neighbouring villages and made a major contribution to the eventual conversion of the area to excellent agricultural land and to the foundation of the town of Wallaceburg.

The Earl of Selkirk and Fort Douglas, heart of the Red River settlement

In 1812 came the undertaking that made the Earl of Selkirk a household name in Canada and Britain and ensured his place in Canadian history. From the Hudson Bay Company he received a grant of land five times the size of Scotland north-west of the Great Lakes and just above the 49th parallel on the Red River in what was to become the prairies. A settlement was established at the junction of the Assiniboine and Red Rivers south of Lake Winnipeg in country which had previously been the preserve of fur traders and local Indians. Access to this remote area was difficult but the natural obstacles were dwarfed by the human ones. The Red River settlement stood on the main trade route of the most powerful and ruthless organization in Canada, the North West Company, fur traders and deadly rivals of the Hudson Bay Company.

Perhaps understandably, but wrongly, the North West Company believed the new settlement was a pretext to cut a vital trade and communications artery and they reacted characteristically to the perceived threat to their existence. Twice Red River was destroyed and the settlers driven out; on the second occasion over twenty settlers were brutally massacred. The danger to his creation brought Selkirk from Britain to play a leading role on the ground. With a contingent of Swiss-German mercenaries and in his capacity as a justice of the peace for Upper Canada he descended on the North West Company's operational headquarters, Fort William on Lake Superior, seized it, arrested the directors there, and sent them back to Montreal for trial.

However he soon discovered how powerful and influential his enemies were. Not only did he fail to have any of them brought to trial but he himself was threatened with arrest for criminal conduct. When he returned to Britain to seek justice for his murdered settlers he discovered the North West Company was no less influential on this side of the Atlantic. Under the stress of events his fragile constitution gave way and he was forced to go abroad to recuperate. But the move was too late and he died in Pau in France in 1820. The Red River colony survived and grew into Winnipeg, capital of Manitoba. But the price had been terrible, the destruction of Selkirk's health and fortune and of the North West Company as an independent organization (weakened and discredited, it had to seek amalgamation with its Hudson Bay rivals).

In Canada Thomas Douglas is regarded as an important contributor to the country's development and recognized accordingly. A town north of Winnipeg and a range of the Rockies both bear his name as do numerous streets and schools. But perhaps his contribution was more important than is conventionally thought. After the 1812 war between Britain and the now independent United States a long dispute rumbled about where the Canada-United States border should run west of the Great Lakes. The American claim that it should be at 54 degrees 40' would have given practically all the great wheat-growing land of the prairies to them but the boundary was eventually fixed at the 49th parallel. Perhaps if Selkirk's Red River settlement had not given Canada a permanent presence in the area with proof of the region's fertility, the British government might not have resisted the United States claims so vigorously. The almost legendary status of the settlement as the colony that would not die may also have been a factor. So it may be that it is thanks to Thomas Douglas from Kirkcudbright that Canada today possesses one of the world's great centres of grain production.

And how is "the Great Earl" commemorated in his home town? A handsome statue to the Earl of Selkirk stands at the crossroads in the centre of Kirkcudbright but the earl in question is not Thomas Douglas but his son. To find the former's memorial you must walk a little further along St Mary St and then look into the Kirk Grounds on your right. There you will see a modest stone plinth about a metre high with a plaque briefly summarising his colonial achievements. It was erected by the Historic Sites Advisory Board of Manitoba in 1978. It seems that in their own country philanthropic colonisers suffer the same fate as prophets.

Sources

| Gray, J. | *Lord Selkirk of Red River* London, 1963 |
| MacKenzie, A. | *Baldoon; Lord Selkirk's Settlement in Upper Canada* Ontario, 1978 |

"POSTIE" HOUSTON, MAN OF MANY PARTS

One of Kirkcudbright's best known residents in the latter part of the nineteenth century and early decades of the twentieth was the remarkable John "Postie" Houston. He enjoyed a national reputation as a weather forecaster and more than local fame for a number of other talents. Born in the town about 1850 and educated at Townhead school, Postie obtained his first job as a farm servant but an accident at work lost him his right hand and part of the arm, forcing a career change. He became a postman on the Kirkcudbright to Borgue round for the rest of his working life, proving a most dedicated employee as his actions during a ferocious snowstorm in 1895 proved. On the first day of the blizzard he was the only person to get in or out of Borgue. On the following days he exchanged his pony and trap for a horse in order to negotiate drifts up to eight feet deep and ensure the mail got through.

His experience on his postal round may have initiated his career in weather forecasting for it gave him ample opportunity to study vast expanses of sky and his method was based on a careful study of the appearance of the sky without recourse to instruments of any kind, a classic "low-tech." procedure. The doings of sun, moon, and tides he considered irrelevant. He claimed accuracy in his forecasts only for four days ahead but within those limits proved so successful that he received mention in several national newspapers and supplied regular forecasts to the Glasgow *Evening Times.* Local people benefited from his skills without payment as he supplied them with predictions from a board outside his house close to the access road to the town cemetery and a pole on which he hoisted coloured balls.

But Postie had other skills. In spite of his physical handicap he excelled at sport, being a fine all-round cricketer and good footballer. He was also a formidable one-mile runner. His footballing interest linked with another notable talent, a facility for mechanical invention. Houston's Time Gun was intended to free referees from their timekeeping duties by automatically signalling half time and full time (presumably in those robust days added-on injury time was unknown). Demonstrations as far away as Glasgow and Liverpool proved its practicability. More commercially significant and well ahead of its time was his automatic coupler for railway wagons, a device which like the time gun sadly was not taken up by the relevant authorities.

Where Postie did enjoy commercial success was in another field of expertise, ratcatching. His services were employed by business organisations all over central and southern Scotland. Here, as in his weather forecasting, his method was pleasingly uncomplicated and highly successful.

During and after his lifetime Postie became a legend for generations of Kirkcudbright residents. Evidence of his fame is his being the subject of at least three picture postcards. These show him to have been a small, dapper man, who sometimes used an artificial arm with a hook attached and favoured fairly formal headgear. His fame posthumously reached the ears of 1930's top travel writer H.V. Morton, who gave him extended coverage (not without inaccuracies) in his book *In Scotland Again*. Even today the name Postie Houston is a familiar one to many local people born long after his multi-talented life was over.

Sources

"Heston"   *John Houston, the Galloway Weather Prophet* <u>in</u> *The Gallovidian,* Spring, 1902

Hunter, J.   personal communication
Millar, Mrs. J.   personal communication

EBENEZER SHAW OF THE HOUSE OF SHAWS

One of Wigtown's most remarkable residents of recent times was Ebenezer Shaw, provost of the burgh for many years in the 1920's and 1930's. Not the least extraordinary fact about him was his possession of three different degrees, in law, medicine, and divinity. Astonishingly, he did not practise any of those vocations, being of independent means. His last home in Wigtown was "Southfield" in South Main Street at the top of the Square. Two of his four daughters were outstanding tennis players, who played for the Wigtown club. Conveniently, the courts were sited in the Square almost opposite the Shaw residence. One of the daughters, Lily, married J. Ridley Brown of the "Galloway Gazette".

Provost Shaw has a claim to literary fame. While at Edinburgh University he became friendly with the famous author Robert Louis Stevenson. Stevenson later conferred a kind of immortality on him by including him in one of the writer's best known books, the children's classic *Kidnapped*, as the rascally uncle of hero David Balfour. Not only has Balfour been deprived of his inheritance by this villain but when he visits him he is almost the victim of a carefully prepared fatal accident and is then kidnapped to be shipped to America. The uncle's name is Ebenezer and his residence, intended scene of Balfour's death, is the House of Shaws. The private joke must have seemed even more appealing in later years when Ebenezer Shaw had become Wigtown's first citizen.

Its appeal would not be diminished by the list of other public offices held by "Uncle Ebenezer": chairman of Wigtownshire Education Committee, honorary sheriff substitute, and justice of the peace for both Wigtownshire and the Stewartry. This last position he held by virtue of his ownership of two estates in that county, Drumrash (his birthplace) near Parton and Bardennoch just south of Carsphairn.

A family tradition says that Ebenezer Shaw knew another famous author, Sir Arthur Conan Doyle, when the two were medical students at Edinburgh University and the chronology supports the claim. It is even just possible that the multi-qualified provost appears in one of Conan Doyle's works for a Wigtown lawyer is mentioned but not named in *The Mystery of Cloomber*.

Sources

Brown, Mrs. A.	Personal communication
Brown, J.R.	personal communication
Galloway Gazette	issue of 13th June, 1935
Melville, Ms. B.	personal communication
Wigtownshire Free Press	issue of 15th June, 1935

VISITS FROM A VIP

Some uncertainty exists about the total number of visits to the Stranraer area paid by Sir Winston Churchill, the great wartime leader. However, it is quite certain that he was there on three occasions, the first attended by a wealth of national publicity and the others in conditions of extreme secrecy.

The initial visit took place in February, 1912, when politics was dominated by two highly controversial questions, those of votes for women and home rule for Ireland. It was the latter which brought Churchill to Stranraer. Asquith's Liberal government was about to introduce a bill granting home rule to the island, a proposal which aroused fierce opposition in Ulster. As First Lord of the Admiralty Churchill was a member of that government and with his customary courage he volunteered to go to Belfast to try to change hearts and minds. Because he was entering the lion's den, his trip was attended by heavy security. Arriving at Stranraer harbour station at 5.45 in the morning on the "Paddy" from London, he went straight on board the Larne ferry *Princess Maud* unattended by either crowd or demonstration.

Matters were much different in Belfast, where his visit was punctuated by hostile demonstrations before, during, and after he addressed an open-air meeting at Celtic Park. Matters were also different at Stranraer when the party returned at 9.50p.m. to board the train for Glasgow. A crowd of several hundred had gathered on the pier to witness his arrival. As the First Lord crossed from the ferry to the station, a woman stepped out of the crowd and struck him in the face with a small, green flag inscribed "No Referendum for Women's Suffrage". For good measure she accompanied her action with the words, not frequently heard at Stranraer station,

"Take that, you cur!"

She was instantly seized and, in the words of the local paper, "roughly pushed aside". However, her unflustered victim interceded on her behalf with the chivalrous plea,

"Don't hurt her, please."

The woman was allowed to go while Churchill and his party proceeded to their train across a crowded platform. In response to demands from the crowd, the First Lord then made a short speech from the compartment window, after which his train departed.

Enquiries revealed that the militant suffragette was not a local resident but a Miss Carmichael of Clement's Inn, The Strand, London. With a female companion she had followed the future prime minister from London to Belfast and back to Stranraer.

As she left on the Paddy to complete her return journey she was the object of much booing from a crowd which did not share her victim's sense of chivalry. The green flag at the centre of the incident fell into the hands of a local postman but sadly its subsequent fate is unrecorded.

Heavy security again and on this occasion total secrecy accompanied Churchill's second visit to Stranraer in June, 1942, en route for Washington and a meeting with President Roosevelt. The Prime Minister, as he now was, again came by rail but this time in a special train, arriving, presumably at the harbour station, in the late evening. From there he was taken by launch to his air transport, a Boeing Clipper flying boat lying at one of RAF Stranraer's moorings, which stretched from the West Pier to the present golf course. Surprisingly this was a civil aircraft belonging to the British Overseas Airways Corporation, which during the war maintained several intercontinental routes. The huge flying boat with its twin decks, crew of eleven, sleeping accommodation for 36 passengers, lounge, and dining salon must have turned a few heads when it appeared in Loch Ryan.

The Prime Minister's brief presence in Stranraer also turned at least two heads. Two local ladies, having completed their voluntary duties at the Services canteen close to the harbour station, were making their separate ways homeward when each saw in the strong light of a late June evening a launch leaving the pier containing the unmistakable figure of Winston Churchill. However they heeded the injunction that "Careless talk costs lives" and unlike Miss Carmichael of The Strand in the same place 30 years earlier had nothing to say in public.

The third Churchill visit took place ten days later when the VIP party returned from Washington. It was a mirror image of its predecessor except for the timing. An early morning arrival in Loch Ryan allowed the party to escape the notice of even the eagle-eyed canteen ladies not to speak of any lurking, latter-day proponents of equal opportunities.

Sources

Anonymous   personal communication

Bridgman, L. (comp.)   *Jane's All the World's Aircraft, 1945; Collector's Edition*
                            London, 1994

Casey, L. <u>and</u> Batchelor, J. *Seaplanes and Flying Boats*   London, 1980

Downie, Mrs J..   personal communication

The *Herald*   issue of 9th February, 2000. Courtesy of R. Bathgate

Murchie, T.   *RAF in Galloway*   Wigtown, 1992

Wigtownshire Free Press   issue of 15th February, 1912

The Boeing Clipper flying boat in which Churchill made his return journey from Loch Ryan to the United States in 1942.

GALLOWAY'S OTHER LINGUISTIC GENIUS

Few writers about Galloway can resist mentioning the remarkable Alexander Murray, largely self-educated shepherd's son from Dunkitterick on the Newton Stewart-New Galloway road, who rose to become Professor of Oriental Languages at Edinburgh University before the flame of his genius was cruelly snuffed out at the age of 37. A prominent monument near his birthplace justly reminds the world of his achievements.

However another locally born linguist of rare ability, whose career shows an astonishing symmetry with Murray's, is virtually unknown and unhonoured. The figure in the shadows is John McGill, who was born at Dunragit near Stranraer in 1832 nineteen years after Murray died. Like the latter he was born into modest circumstances: his father was carpenter for the Dalrymple Hay family at Dunragit House on their Park-Dunragit estate. His mother was the daughter of a farmer in the parish of Kirkcolm. The laird must have valued his house carpenter highly perhaps because he was also a crew member on the Dalrymple Hay yacht, *Sappho*. At any rate when James McGill married, a cottage was built on the estate for the couple and furnished.

The McGills had four sons, all of whom were educated at the local school, Drochduil, which had been founded and was supported by the ladies of the Dalrymple Hay family. This was not the present school at the side of the A715 Whitecrook to Sandhead road south of Dunragit but was located about two hundred metres to the north. The site now lies in a wood but the school foundations are still clearly visible. Drochduil must have provided a good education because three of the McGill sons distinguished themselves in later life. One became a successful London doctor and another, more exotically, was principal engineer to the Turkish navy. However our concern is with the eldest son, John. His path to university was easier than Murray's thanks to a school bursary presented by Lord Bute. Unlike Murray his choice was Glasgow but there, like the Dunkitterick man at Edinburgh, he studied languages and particularly oriental languages.

The parallels between the two men continue in their choice of career, both opting for the ministry. But while Murray returned to a Galloway parish, Urr in the Stewartry, McGill went to Sauchie in Clackmannanshire. The final career symmetry seems almost to belong to the realms of fiction. Just as Murray had been appointed to Edinburgh University's Chair of Oriental Languages so McGill was chosen as Professor of Hebrew and Oriental Languages at St Andrews University. And just as the early nineteenth century had seen a Galloway man hailed as the finest oriental scholar in Britain, if not in Europe, so fifty years later a Galloway man was again granted that accolade, this time by no less an authority than the famous Oxford Unversity divine Dr Pusey.

But neither man's story was to have a happy ending. The concluding similarity between the two academic giants is a deeply sad one. Alexander Murray died of tuberculosis at the age of only thirty-seven; John McGill was granted just one year more. He was one of the few Scots clergymen appointed to a committee given the formidable task of revising the Authorized Version of the Bible. On his way home by sea from a meeting in London he contracted dysentery and died soon afterwards. Neither is buried in his native Galloway but both have appropriately distinguished resting places, Professor Murray D.D. in Edinburgh's Greyfriars churchyard under a monument of Dalbeattie granite and Professor McGill L.L.D. in the cathedral burial ground in St Andrews.

Here in Galloway Alexander Murray is properly commemorated in literature and in stone. John McGill has only an inscription added to his father's headstone in Glenluce old churchyard, recording the bare facts of his life. He deserves better.

Sources

Dalrymple Hay, J.	*Lines from My Log-Books*	Edinburgh, 1898
Wigtownshire Free Press	issues of March, 1871	

A 1920's view of Dunragit House, where John McGill's father was house carpenter.